Stained Glass

(Illustrated Edition)

By

C. W. Whall

The Echo Library 2010

Published by

The Echo Library

Unit 22
Horcott Industrial Estate
Horcott Road
Fairford
Glos. GL7 4BX

www.echo-library.com

ISBN 978-1-4068-6843-2

"...And remembering these, trust Pindar for the truth of his saying, that to the cunning workman—(and let me solemnly enforce the words by adding, that to him only)—knowledge comes undeceitful."

—RUSKIN ("Aratra Pentelici").

"'Very cool of Tom,' as East thought but didn't say, 'seeing as how he only came out of Egypt himself last night at bed-time.'"

—("Tom Brown's Schooldays").

THE ARTISTIC CRAFTS SERIES OF TECHNICAL HANDBOOKS
EDITED BY W. R. LETHABY

STAINED GLASS WORK

CUTTING AND GLAZING
Frontispiece

STAINED GLASS WORK

A TEXT-BOOK FOR STUDENTS AND WORKERS IN GLASS.

BY

C. W. WHALL.

WITH DIAGRAMS BY TWO OF HIS APPRENTICES
AND OTHER ILLUSTRATIONS

NEW YORK
D. APPLETON AND COMPANY
MCMXIV

Printed by BALLANTYNE, HANSON & CO.
at the Ballantyne Press, Edinburgh

To his Pupils and Assistants, who, if they have learned as much from him as he has from them, have spent their time profitably; and who, if they have enjoyed learning as much as he has teaching, have spent it happily; this little book is Dedicated by their Affectionate Master and Servant,

THE AUTHOR.

EDITOR'S PREFACE

In issuing these volumes of a series of Handbooks on the Artistic Crafts, it will be well to state what are our general aims.

In the first place, we wish to provide trustworthy text-books of workshop practice, from the points of view of experts who have critically examined the methods current in the shops, and putting aside up a standard of quality in the crafts which are more especially associated with design. Secondly, in doing this, we hope to treat design itself as an essential part of good workmanship. During the last century most of the arts, save painting and sculpture of an academic kind, were little considered, and there was a tendency to look on "design" as a mere matter of *appearance*. Such "ornamentation" as there was usually obtained by following in a mechanical way a drawing provided by an artist who often knew little of the technical processes involved in production. With the critical attention given to the crafts by Ruskin and Morris, it came to be seen that it was impossible to detach design from craft in this way, and that, in the widest sense, true design is an inseparable element of good quality, involving as it does the selection of good and suitable material, contrivance for special purpose, expert workmanship, proper finish, and so on, far more than mere ornament, and indeed, that ornamentation itself was rather an exuberance of fine workmanship than a matter of merely abstract lines. Workmanship when separated by too wide a gulf from fresh thought—that is, from design—inevitably decays, and, on the other hand, ornamentation, divorced from workmanship, is necessarily unreal, and quickly falls into affectation. Proper ornamentation may be defined as a language addressed to the eye; it is pleasant thought expressed in the speech of the tool.

In the third place, we would have this series put artistic craftsmanship before people as furnishing reasonable occupations for those who would gain a livelihood. Although within the bounds of academic art, the competition, of its kind, is so acute that only a very few per cent. can fairly hope to succeed as painters and sculptors; yet, as artistic craftsmen, there is every probability that nearly every one who would pass through a sufficient period of apprenticeship to workmanship and design would reach a measure of success.

In the blending of handwork and thought in such arts as we propose to deal with, happy careers may be found as far removed from the dreary routine of hack labour as from the terrible uncertainty of academic art. It is desirable in every way that men of good education should be brought back into the productive crafts: there are more than enough of us "in the city," and it is probable that more consideration will be given in this century than in the last to Design and Workmanship.

Our last volume dealt with one of the branches of sculpture, the present treats of one of the chief forms of painting. Glass-painting has been, and is capable of again becoming, one of the most noble forms of Art. Because of its subjection to strict conditions, and its special glory of illuminated colour, it holds a supreme position in its association with architecture, a position higher than any other art, except, perhaps, mosaic and sculpture.

The conditions and aptitudes of the Art are most suggestively discussed in the present volume by one who is not only an artist, but also a master craftsman. The great question of colour has been here opened up for the first time in our series, and it is well that it should be so, in connection with this, the pre-eminent colour-art.

Windows of coloured glass were used by the Romans. The thick lattices found in Arab art, in which brightly-coloured morsels of glass are set, and upon which the idea of the jewelled windows in the story of Aladdin is doubtless based, are Eastern off-shoots from this root.

Painting in line and shade on glass was probably invented in the West not later than the year 1100, and there are in France many examples, at Chartres, Le Mans, and other places, which date back to the middle of the twelfth century.

Theophilus, the twelfth-century writer on Art, tells us that the French glass was the most famous. In England the first notice of stained glass is in connection with Bishop Hugh's work at Durham, of which we are told that around the altar he placed several glazed windows remarkable for the beauty of the figures which they contained; this was about 1175.

In the Fabric Accounts of our national monuments many interesting facts as to mediæval stained glass are preserved. The accounts of the building of St. Stephen's Chapel, in the middle of the fourteenth century, make known to us the procedure of the mediæval craftsmen. We find in these first a workman preparing white boards, and then the master glazier drawing the cartoons on the whitened boards, and many other details as to customs, prices, and wages.

There is not much old glass to be studied in London, but in the museum at South Kensington there are specimens of some of the principal varieties. These are to be found in the Furniture corridor and the corridor which leads from it. Close by a fine series of English coats of arms of the fourteenth century, which are excellent examples of Heraldry, is placed a fragment of a broad border probably of late twelfth-century work. The thirteenth century is represented by a remarkable collection, mostly from the Ste. Chapelle in Paris and executed about 1248. The most striking of these remnants show a series of Kings seated amidst bold scrolls of foliage, being parts of a Jesse Tree, the narrower strips, in which are Prophets, were placed to the right and left of the Kings, and all three made up the width of one light in the original window. The deep brilliant colour, the small pieces of glass used, and the rich backgrounds are all characteristic of mid-thirteenth-century glazing. Of early fifteenth-century workmanship are the large single figures standing under canopies, and these are good examples of English glass of this time. They were removed from Winchester College Chapel about 1825 by the process known as restoration.

W. R. LETHABY.

January 1905.

AUTHOR'S PREFACE

The author must be permitted to explain that he undertook his task with some reluctance, and to say a word by way of explaining his position.

I have always held that no art can be taught by books, and that an artist's best way of teaching is directly and personally to his own pupils, and maintained these things stubbornly and for long to those who wished this book written. But I have such respect for the good judgment of those who have, during the last eight years, worked in the teaching side of the art and craft movement, and, in furtherance of its objects, have commenced this series of handbooks, and such a belief in the movement, of which these persons and circumstances form a part, that I felt bound to yield on the condition of saying just what I liked in my own way, and addressing myself only to students, speaking as I would speak to a class or at the bench, careless of the general reader.

You will find yourself, therefore, reader, addressed as "Dear Student." (I know the term occurs further on.) But because this book is written for students, it does not therefore mean that it must all be brought within the comprehension of the youngest apprentice. For it is becoming the fashion, in our days, for artists of merit—painters, perhaps, even of distinction—to take up the practice of one or other of the crafts. All would be well, for such new workers are needed, if it was indeed the *practice* of the craft that they set themselves to. But too often it is what is called the *designing* for it only in which they engage, and it is the duty of every one speaking or writing about the matter to point out how fatal is that error.

One must provide a word, then, for such as these also here if one can.

Indeed, to reckon up all the classes to whom such a book as this should be addressed, we should have, I think, to name:—(1) The worker in the ordinary "shop," who is learning there at present, to our regret, only a portion of his craft, and who should be given an insight into the whole, and into the fairyland of design.

(2) The magnificent and superior artist, mature in imagination and composition, fully equipped as a painter of pictures, perhaps even of academical distinction, who turns his attention to the craft, and without any adequate practical training in it, which alone could teach its right principles, makes, and in the nature of things is bound to make, great mistakes—mistakes easily avoidable. No such thing can possibly be right. Raphael himself designed for tapestry, and the cartoons are priceless, but the tapestry a ghastly failure. It could not have been otherwise under the conditions. Executant separated from designer by all the leagues that lie between Arras and Rome.

(3) The patron, who should know something of the craft, that he may not, mistrusting, as so often at present, his own taste, be compelled to trust to some one else's Name, and of course looks out for a big one.

(4) The architect and church dignitary who, having such grave responsibilities in their hands towards the buildings of which they are the guardians, wish, naturally, to understand the details which form a part of their

charge. And lastly, a new and important class that has lately sprung into existence, the well-equipped, picked student—brilliant and be-medalled, able draughtsman, able painter; young, thoughtful, ambitious, and educated, who, instead of drifting, as till recently, into the overcrowded ranks of picture-making, has now the opportunity of choosing other weapons in the armoury of the arts.

To all these classes apply those golden words from Ruskin's "Aratra Pentelici" which are quoted on the fly-leaf of the present volume, while the spirit in which I myself would write in amplifying them is implied by my adopting the comment and warning expressed in the other sentence there quoted. The face of the arts is in a state of change. The words "craft" and "craftsmanship," unheard a decade or two ago, now fill the air; we are none of us inheritors of any worthy tradition, and those who have chanced to grope about for themselves, and seem to have found some safe footing, have very little, it seems to me, to plume or pride themselves upon, but only something to be thankful for in their good luck. But "to have learnt faithfully" one of the "ingenuous arts" (or crafts) *is* good luck and *is* firm footing; we may not doubt it who feel it strong beneath our feet, and it must be proper to us to help towards it the doubtless quite as worthy or worthier, but less fortunate, who may yet be in some of the quicksands around.

It also happens that the art of stained glass, though reaching to very high and great things, is in its methods and processes a simple, or at least a very limited, one. There are but few things to do, while at the same time the principles of it touch the whole field of art, and it is impossible to treat of it without discussing these great matters and the laws which guide decorative art generally. It happens conveniently, therefore, as the technical part requires less space, that these things should be treated of in this particular book, and it becomes the author's delicate and difficult task to do so. He, therefore, wishes to make clear at starting the spirit in which the task is undertaken.

It remains only to express his thanks to Mr. Drury and Mr. Noel Heaton for help respectively, with the technical and scientific detail; to Mr. St. John Hope for permission to use his reproductions from the Windsor stall-plates, and to Mr. Selwyn Image for his great kindness in revising the proofs.

C. W. WHALL.

January 1905.

CONTENTS

PART I

CHAPTER I

INTRODUCTORY, AND CONCERNING THE RAW MATERIAL

You are to know that stained glass means pieces of coloured glasses put together with strips of lead into the form of windows; not a picture painted on glass with coloured paints.

You know that a beer bottle is blackish, a hock bottle orange-brown, a soda-water bottle greenish-white—these are the colours of the whole substance of which they are respectively made.

Break such a bottle, each little bit is still a bit of coloured glass. So, also, blue is used for poison bottles, deep green and deep red for certain wine glasses, and, indeed, almost all colours for one purpose or another.

Now these are the same glass, and coloured in the same way as that used for church windows.

Such coloured glasses are cut into the shapes of faces, or figures, or robes, or canopies, or whatever you want and whatever the subject demands; then features are painted on the faces, folds on the robes, and so forth—not with colour, merely with brown shading; then, when this shading has been burnt into the glass in a kiln, the pieces are put together into a picture by means of grooved strips of lead, into which they fit.

This book, it is hoped, will set forth plainly how these things are done, for the benefit of those who do not know; and, for the benefit of those who do know, it will examine and discuss the right principles on which windows should be made, and the rules of good taste and of imagination, which make such a difference between beautiful and vulgar art; for you may know intimately all the processes I have spoken of, and be skilful in them, and yet misapply them, so that your window had better never have been made.

Skill is good if you use it wisely and for good end; but craft of hand employed foolishly is no more use to you tan swiftness of foot would be upon the broad road leading downwards—the cripple is happier.

A clear and calculating brain may be used for statesmanship or science, or merely for gambling. You, we will say, have a true eye and a cunning hand; will you use them on the passing fashion of the hour—the morbid, the trivial, the insincere—or in illustrating the eternal truths and dignities, the heroisms and sanctities of life, and its innocencies and gaieties?

This book, then, is divided into two parts, of which the intention of one is to promote and produce skilfulness of hand, and of the other to direct it to worthy ends.

The making of glass itself—of the raw material—the coloured glasses used in stained-glass windows, cannot be treated of here. What are called "Antiques" are chiefly used, and there are also special glasses representing the ideals and

16

experiments of enthusiasts—Prior's "Early English" glass, and the somewhat similar "Norman" glass. These glasses, however, are for craftsmen of experience to use: they require mature skill and judgment in the using; to the beginner, "Antiques" are enough for many a day to come.

How to know the Right and Wrong Sides of a Piece of "Antique" Glass.—Take up a sheet of one of these and look at it. You will notice that the two sides look different; one side has certain little depressions as if it had been pricked with a pin, sometimes also some wavy streaks. Turn it round, and, looking at the other side, you still see these things, but blurred, as if seen through water, while the surface itself on this side looks smooth; what inequalities there are being projections rather than depressions. Now the side you first looked at is the side to cut on, and the side to paint on, and it is the side placed inwards when the window is put up.

The reason is this. Glass is made into sheets by being blown into bubbles, just as a child blows soap-bubbles. If you blow a soap-bubble you will see streaks playing about in it, just like the wavy streaks you notice in the glass.

The bubble is blown, opened at the ends, and manipulated with tools while hot, until it is the shape of a drain-pipe; then cut down one side and opened out upon a flattening-stone until the round pipe is a flat sheet; and it is this stone which gives the glass the different texture, the dimpled surface which you notice.

Some glasses are "flashed"; that is to say, a bubble is blown which is mainly composed of white glass; but, before blowing, it is also dipped into another coloured glass—red, perhaps, or blue—and the two are then blown together, so that the red or blue glass spreads out into a thin film closely united to, in fact fused on to, and completely one with, the white glass which forms the base; most "Ruby" glasses are made in this way.

CHAPTER II

Cutting (elementary)—The Diamond—The Wheel—Sharpening—How to Cut—Amount of Force— The Beginner's Mistake—Tapping— Possible and Impossible Cuts—"Grozeing"—Defects of the Wheel—The Actual Nature of a "Cut" in Glass.

No written directions can teach the use of the diamond; it is as sensitive to the hand as the string of a violin, and a good workman feels with a most delicate touch exactly where the cutting edge is, and uses his tool accordingly. Every apprentice counts on spoiling a guinea diamond in the learning, which will take him from one to two years.

Most cutters now use the wheel, of which illustrations are given (figs. 1 and 2).

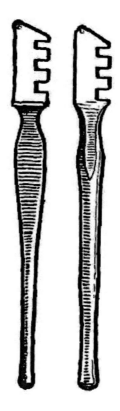

FIGS. 1 and 2.

The wheels themselves are good things, and cut as well as the diamond, in some respects almost better; but many of the handles are very unsatisfactory.

From some of them indeed one might suppose, if such a thing were conceivable, that the maker knew nothing of the use of the tool.

For it is held thus (fig. 5), the pressure of the *forefinger* both guiding the cut and supplying force for it: and they give you an *edge* to press on (fig. 1) instead of a surface! In some other patterns, indeed, they do give you the desired surface, but the tool is so thin that there is nothing to grip. What ought to be done is to reproduce the shape of the old wooden handle of the diamond proper (figs. 3 and 4).

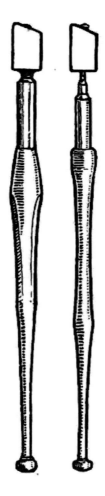

FIGS. 3 and 4.

The foregoing passage must, however, be amplified and modified, but this I will do further on, for you will understand the reasons better if I insert it after what I had written further with regard to the cutting of glass.

How to Sharpen the Wheel Cutter.—The right way to do this is difficult to describe in writing. You must, first of all, grind down the "shoulders" of the tool, through which the pivot of the wheel goes, for they are made so large that the wheel cannot reach the stone (fig. 6), and must be reduced (fig. 7). Then, after first oiling the pivot so that the wheel may run easily, you must hold the tool as shown in fig. 8, and rub it swiftly up and down the stone. The angle at which the wheel should rest on the stone is shown in fig. 9. You will see that the angle at which the wheel meets the stone is a little *blunter* than the angle of the side of the wheel itself. You do not want to make the tool *too sharp*, otherwise you will risk breaking down the edge, when the wheel will cease to be truly circular, and when that occurs it is absolutely useless. The same thing will happen if the wheel is *checked* in its revolution while sharpening, and therefore the pivot must be kept oiled both for cutting and sharpening.

FIG. 5.

It is a curious fact to notice that the tool, be it wheel or diamond, that is *too sharp* is not, in practice, found to make so good a cut as one that is less sharp; it scratches the glass and throws up a line of splinters.

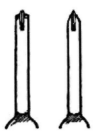

FIGS. 6 and 7.

FIG. 8.

How to Cut Glass.—Hold the cutter as shown in the illustration (fig. 5), a little sloping towards you, but perfectly upright laterally; draw it towards you, hard enough to make it just *bite* the glass. If it leaves a mark you can hardly see it is a good cut (fig. 10B), but if it scratches a white line, throwing up glass-dust as it goes, either the tool is faulty, or you are pressing too hard, or you are applying the pressure to the wheel unevenly and at an angle to the direction of the cut (fig. 10A). Not that you can make the wheel *move* sideways in the cut actually; it will keep itself straight as a ploughshare keeps in its furrow, but it will press sideways, and so break down the edges of the furrow, while if you exaggerate this enough it will actually leave the furrow, and, ceasing to cut, will "skid" aside over the glass. As to pressure, all cutters begin by pressing much too hard; the tool having started biting, it should be kept only *just biting* while drawn along. The cut should be almost *noiseless*. You think you're not cutting because you don't hear it grate, but hold the glass sideways to the light and you will see the silver line quite continuous.

Having made your cut, take the glass up; hold it as in fig. 11, press downward with the thumbs and upward with the fingers, and the glass will come apart.

FIG. 9.

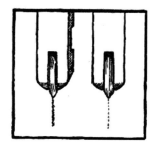

FIG. 10, A and B

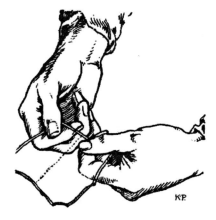

FIG. 11.

But you want to cut shaped pieces as well as straight. You cannot break these directly the cut is made, but, holding the glass as in fig. 12, and pressing it firmly with the left thumb, jerk the tool up by little, sharp jerks of the fingers *only*, so as to tap along the underside of your cut. You will see a little silver line spring along the cut, showing that the glass is dividing; and when that silver line has sprung from end to end, a gentle pressure will bring the glass apart.

FIG. 12.

This upward jerk must be sharp and swift, but must be calculated so as only just to *reach* the glass, being checked just at the right point, as one hammers a *nail* when one does not want to stir the work into which the nail is driven. A *pushing* stroke, a blow that would go much further if the glass were not there, is no use; and for this reason neither the elbow nor the hand must move; the knuckles are the hinge upon which the stroke revolves.

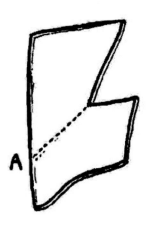

FIG. 13.

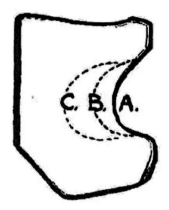

FIG. 14.

But you can only cut certain shapes—for instance, you cannot cut a wedge-shaped gap out of a piece of glass (fig. 13); however tenderly you handle it, it will split at point A. The nearest you can go to it is a curve; and the deeper the curve the more difficult it is to get the piece out. In fig. 14 A is an average easy curve, B a difficult one, C impossible, except by "groseing" or "grozeing" as cutters call it; that is, after the cut is made, setting to work to patiently bite the piece out with pliers (fig. 15).

FIG. 15.

Now, further, you must understand that you must not cut round all the sides of a shaped piece of glass at once; indeed, you must only cut one side at a time, and draw your cut right up to the edge of the glass, and break away the whole piece which *contains* the side you are cutting before you go on to another.

Thus, in fig. 16, suppose the shaded portion to be the shape that you wish to cut out of the piece of glass, A, B, C, D. You must lay your gauge *anglewise* down upon the piece. Do not try to get the sides parallel to the shapes of your gauge, for that makes it much more difficult; angular pieces break off the easiest.

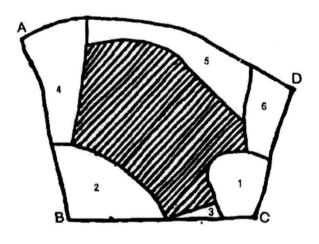

FIG. 16.

Now, then, *cut the most difficult piece first*. That marked 1. Perhaps you will not cut it quite true; but, if not, then shift the gauge slightly on to another part of the curve, and very likely it may fit that better and so *come* true.

Then follow with one of those marked 2 or 3. Probably it would be safest to cut the larger and more difficult piece first, and get *both* the curved cuts right by your gauge; then you can be quite sure of getting the very easy small bit off quite truly, to fit into its place with both of them. Go on with 4, and then with one of those marked 5 or 6. Probably it would still be best to cut the curved piece first, unless you think that shortening it by cutting off the small corner-piece first will make the curved cut easier by making it shorter.

In any case you must only cut one side at a time, and break it away before you make the cut for another side.

Take care that you do not go back in your cut. You must try and make it quite continuous onwards; for if you go back in the cut, where your tool has already thrown up splinters, it will spoil your tool and spoil your cut also.

Difficult curves, that it is only just possible to get out by groseing, ought never to be resorted to, except for some very sufficient reason. A cartoonist who knows the craft will avoid setting such tasks to the cutter; but, unfortunately, many cartoonists do *not* know the craft. If people were taught the complete craft as they should be, this book would not have been written.

Here let me say that we cannot possibly within the narrow limits of it go thoroughly into all the very wide range of subjects connected with glass—the chemistry, the permanence, the purity of materials. With the exception of the practice of the craft, probably we shall not be able to go thoroughly into any one of them; but I shall endeavour to *mention* them all, and to do so sufficiently to indicate the directions in which work and research and experiment may be made, for they are all three much needed in several directions.

It becomes, for instance, now my task, in modifying the passage some pages back as I promised, to go into one of these subjects in the light of inquiries made since the passage in question was written; and I let it for the time being stand just as it was, without the additional information, because it gives a picture of how such things crop up and of the way in which such investigations may be made, and of how useful and pleasant they may be.

Here then let us have—

A LITTLE DISSERTATION UPON CUTTING.

Through the agent for the wheel-cutter in England I communicated with the maker and inventor in America, and told him of our difficulties and perplexities over here, and chiefly with regard to two points. First, the awkwardness of the handle, which causes the glaziers here to use the tool bound round with wadding, or enclosed in a bit of india-rubber pipe; and, secondly, the bluntness of the "jaws" which hold the wheel, and which must be ground down (and are in universal practice ground down), before the tool can be sharpened.

His reply called attention to a number of different patterns of handle, the existence of which, I think, is not generally known, in England at any rate, and some of which seem to more or less meet the difficulties we experience, most of them also being made with malleable iron handles, so that fresh cutting-wheels can be inserted in the same handle. His letter also entered into the question of the actual dynamics of "cutting," maintaining, I think rightly, that a "cut" is made by the edge of the wheel (this not being very sharp) forcing the particles of the glass down into the mass of it by pressure.

With regard to the old-fashioned pattern of tool which we chiefly use in this country, the very sufficient explanation is that they continue to make it because we continue to demand it, a circumstance which, as he declares, is a mystery to the inventor himself! Nevertheless, as we do so, and, in spite of the variety of newer tools on the market, still go on grinding down the jaws of our favourite, and wrapping round the handle with cotton-wool, let us try and put this matter straight, and compare our requirements with the advantages offered us.

There are three chief points to be cleared up. (1) The actual nature of a "cut" in glass; (2) the question of sharpening the tool and grinding down of the jaws to do so; and (3) the "mystery" of our preference for a particular tool, although we all confess its awkwardness by the means we take to modify it.

(1) With regard, then, to the nature of a "cut" in glass I am disposed entirely to agree with the theory put forward by the inventor of the wheel, which an examination of the cuts under the microscope, or even a 6 diameter lens, certainly also tends to confirm.

What happens appears to my non-scientific eyes to be this.

Glass is one of the most fissile or "splittable" of all materials; but it is so just in the same way that ice is, and just in the opposite way to that in which slate or talc is.

Slate or talc splits easily into thin layers or laminæ, *because it already lies in such layers*, and these will come apart when the force is applied between them: but *it will only split into the laminæ of which it already is composed, and along the line of the fissures which already exist between them.*

Glass, on the contrary (and the same is true of ice, or for that matter of currant-jelly and such like things), appears to be a substance which is the same in all directions, or nearly so, and therefore as liable to split in one direction as in another, and is so loosely held together that, once a splitting force is applied, the crack spreads very rapidly and easily, and therefore smoothly and in straight lines and in even planes.

The diamond, or the wheel-cutter, is such a force. Being pressed on to the surface, it forces down the particles, and these start a series of small vertical splits, sometimes nearly through the whole thickness of the glass, though invisibly so until the glass is separated. And mark, that it is the *starting* of the splits that is the important thing; there is no object in making them *deep*, it is only wasted force; they will continue to split of themselves if encouraged in the proper way (see Plates IX. and X.). Try this as follows.

Take a bit of glass, say 3 inches by 2, and make the very smallest dint you can in it, in the middle of the narrowest dimension. You cannot make one so small that the glass will hold together if you try to break it across. It will break across in a straight line, springing from each end of the tiny cut. The cut may be only 1/8 of an inch long; less—it may be only 1/16, 1/32—as small as you will, the glass will break across just the same.

Why?

Because the cut has *started* it splitting at each end; and the material being the same all through, the split will go straight on in the direction in which it has started; there is nothing to turn it aside.

So also the pressure of the wheel starts a continuous split, or series of splits, *downwards*, into the thickness of the glass. No matter how small a distance these go in, the glass will come asunder directly pressure is applied.

Now, if you press too hard in cutting, another thing takes place.

Imagine a quantity of roofing-slates piled flat one on top of another, all the piles being of equal height and arranged in two rows, side by side, so close that the edges of the slates in one row touch the edges of those in the other row, along a central line.

Wheel a wheelbarrow along that line over the edges of both.

What would happen?

The top layer of slates would all come cocking their outer edges up as the barrow passed over their inner ones, would they not?

Now, just so, if you press hard on your glass-cutting wheel, it will press down the edges of the groove, and though there are no layers *already made* in the glass, the pressure will *split off* a thin layer from the top surface of the glass on each side in flakes as it goes along (Plate X., D, E).

This is what gives the *noise* of the cut, c-r-r-r-r-; and as the thing is no use the noise is no use; like a good many other things in life, the less noise the better work, much cry generally meaning little wool, as the man found out who shaved the pig.

But the wheel or the diamond is not quite the same as the wheel of the wheelbarrow, for it has a *wedge-shaped* edge. Imagine a barrow with such a wheel; what *then* would happen to your slates? besides being cocked up by the wheel, they would also be *pushed out*, surely?

This happens in glass. You must not imagine that glass is a rigid thing; it is very elastic, and the wedge-like pressure of the wheel pushes it out just as the keel of a boat pushes the water aside in ripples (Plate X., D, E).

All these observations seem to me to bear out the theory of the inventor, and perhaps to some extent to explain it. I am much tempted to carry them further, and ask the questions, why a penknife as well as a wheel will not make a cut in glass, but will make a perfectly definite scratch on it if the glass is placed under water? and why this line so made will yet not serve for separating the glass? and why a piece of glass can be cut in two (roughly, to be sure, but still cut in two) with a pair of scissors under water, a thing otherwise quite impossible?

But I do not think that the knowledge of these questions will help the reader to do better stained-glass windows, and therefore I will not pursue them.

(2) The question of sharpening the tool is soon disposed of.

If the tool is to be sharpened, the jaws must be ground down, whether the maker grinds them down originally or whether we do it. Is sharpening worth while, since the tool only costs a few pence?

Well, it's a question each must decide for himself; but I will just answer two small difficulties which affect the matter.

If grinding the jaws loosens the pivot, it can be hammered tight again with a punch. If sharpening wears out the oil-stone (as it undoubtedly does, and oil-stones are expensive things), a piece of fine polished Westmoreland slate will do as well, and there is no need to be chary of it. Even a piece of ground-glass with oil will do.

(3) But now as to the handle. I am first to explain the amusing "mystery" why the old pattern shown in fig. 1 still sells.

It is because the British working-man *is convinced that the wheels in this handle are better quality than any others.*

Is he right, or is it only an instance of his love for and faith in the thing he has got used to?

Or can it be that all workmen do not know of the existence of the other types of handle? In case this is so, I figure some (fig. 17). Or is it that the wheel for some reason runs less truly in the malleable iron than in the cast iron?

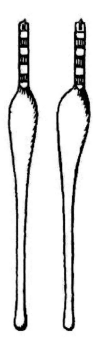

FIG. 17.

Certain it is that the whole trade here prefers these wheels, and I am bound to say that as far as my experience goes they seem to me to work better than those in other handles.

But as to all the handles themselves, I must now voice our general complaint.

(1) They are too light.

For tapping our heavy antique and slab-glasses we wish we had a heavier tool.

(2) They are too thin in the handle for comfort, at least it seems so to me.

(3) The three gashes cut out of the head of the tool decrease the weight, and if these were omitted the tool would gain. Their only use that I can conceive of is that of a very poor substitute for pliers as a "groseing" tool, if one has forgotten one's pliers. But (as Serjeant Buzfuz might say) "who *does* forget his pliers?"

The whole question of the handle is complicated by the fact that some cutters rest the tool on the forefinger and some on the middle finger in tapping, and that a handle the sections of which are calculated for the one will not do equally well for the other.

But the whole thing resolves itself into this, that if we could get a tool, the handle of which corresponded in all its curves, dimensions, and sections with the old-established diamond, I think we should all be glad; and if the head, wheel, and pivot were all made of the quality and material of which fig. 1 is now made, but with the handle as I describe, many of us, I think, would be still more glad; and if these remarks lead in any degree to such results, they at least of all the book will have been worth the writing, and will probably be its best claim to a white stone in Israel, as removing one more solecism from "this so-called twentieth century."

I shall now leave this subject of cutting for the present, and describe, up to about the same point, the processes of painting, taking both on to a higher stage later—as if, in fact, I were teaching a pupil; for as soon as you can cut glass well enough to cut a piece to paint on, you should learn to paint on it, and carry the two things on step by step, side by side.

CHAPTER III

Painting (elementary)—Pigments—Mixing—How to Fill the Brush—
Outline—Examples—Industry—The Needle and Stick—Completing the
Outline.

The pigments for painting on glass are powders, being the oxides of various
minerals, chiefly iron. There are others; but take it thus—that the iron oxide is a
red pigment, and the others are introduced, mainly, to modify this. The red
pigment is the best to use, and goes off less in the firing; but, alas! it is a detestably
ugly *colour*, like red lead; and, do what you will, you cannot use it on white glass.
Against clear sky it looks pretty well in some lights, but get it in a sidelight, or at
an angle, and the whole window looks like red brick; while, seen against any
background except clear sky, it always looks so from all points of view. There are
various makers of these pigments. Some glass-painters make their own, and a
beginner with any knowledge of chemistry would be wise to work in that
direction.

FIG. 18.

I need not discuss the various kinds of pigment; what follows is a description
of my own practice in the matter.

To Mix the Pigment for Painting.—Take a teaspoonful of red tracing-colour, and a rather smaller spoonful of intense black, put them on a slab of thick ground-glass about 9 inches square, and drop clean water upon them till you can work them up into a paste with the palette-knife (fig. 18); work them up for a minute or so, till the paste is smooth and the lumps broken up, and then add about three drops of strong gum made from the purest white gum-arabic dissolved in cold water. Any good chemist will sell this, but its purity is a matter of great importance, for you want the maximum of adhesiveness with the minimum of the material.

Mix the colour well up with the knife; then take one of those long-haired sable brushes, which are called "riggers" (fig. 19), and which all artists'-colourmen sell, and fill it with the colour, diluting it with enough water to make it quite thin. Do not dilute all the pigment; keep most of it in a tidy lump, merely moist, as you ground it and not further wetted, at the corner of your slab; but always keep a portion diluted in a small "pond" in the middle of your palette.

How to Fill the Brush with Pigment.—Now you must note that this is a heavy powder floating free in water, therefore it quickly sinks to the bottom of your little "pond." *Each time you fill your brush you must "stir up the mud,"* for the "mud" is what you want to get in your brush, and not only so, but you want to get your brush *evenly full* of it from tip to base, therefore you must splay out the hairs flat against the glass, till all are wet, and then in taking it off the palette, "twiddle" it to a point quickly. This takes long to describe, but it does not take a couple of seconds to do. You must have the patience to spend so much pains on it, and even to fill the brush very often, nearly for each touch; then you will get a clear, smooth, manageable stroke for your outline, and save time in the end.

FIG. 19.

How to Paint in Outline.—Make some strokes (fig. 20) on a piece of glass and let them dry; some people like them to stick very tight to the glass, some so that a touch of the finger removes them; you must find which suits you by-and-by, and vary the amount of gum accordingly; but to begin, I would advise that they should be just removable by a moderately hard rub with the finger, rather less hard a rub than you close a gummed envelope with.

Practise now for a time the making of strokes, large and small, dark and light, broad and fine; and when you have got command of your tools, set yourself the task of doing the same thing, *copying an example placed underneath your bit of glass.* You will find a hand-rest (fig. 21) an assistance in this.

FIG. 20.

It is difficult to give any list of examples suitable for this stage of glass, but the kind of line employed on the best *heraldry* is always good for the purpose. The splendid illustrations of this in Mr. St. John-Hope's book of the stall-plates of the Knights of the Garter at Windsor, examples of which by the author's courtesy I am allowed to reproduce (figs. 22-22A), are ideal for bold outline-work, and fascinatingly interesting for their own sake. In most of these there is not only excellent practice in *outline*, and a great deal of it, but, mixed with it, practice also in flat washes, which it is a good thing to be learning side by side with the other.

And here let me note that there are throughout the practice of glass-painting *many* methods in use at every stage. Each person, each firm of glass-stainers, has his own methods and traditions. I shall not trouble to notice all these as we come to them, but describe what seems to me to be the best practice in each case; but I shall here and there give a word about others.

FIG. 21.

For instance: if you use sugar or treacle instead of gum, you get a rather smoother-working pigment, and after it is dry you can moisten it as often as you will for further work by merely breathing on the surface; and perhaps if your aim is *outline only*, it may be well to try it; but if you wish to pass shading-colour over it you must use gum, for you cannot do so over treacle colour; nor do I think treacle serves so well for the next process I am to describe, which here follows.

FIG. 22.

How to complete the Outline better than you possibly can by One Tracing.—When you take up a bit of glass from the table, after having done all you can to make a correct tracing, you will be disappointed with the result. It will have looked pretty well on the table with the copy showing behind it and hiding its defects, but it is a different thing when held up to the searching daylight. This must not, however, discourage you. No one, not the most skilful, could expect to make a perfect copy of an original (if that original had any fineness of line or sensitiveness of touch about it) by merely tracing it downwards on the bench. You must put it upright against the daylight, and mend your drawing, freehand, faithfully by the copy.

FIG. 22A.

These remarks do not, in a great degree, apply to the case of hard outlines specially prepared for literal translation. I am speaking of those where the outline is, in the artistic sense, sensitive and refined, as in a Botticelli painting or a Holbein drawing, and to copy these well you want an easel.

For this small work any kind of frame with a sheet of glass in it, and a ledge to rest your bit of glass on and a leg to stand out behind, will do, and by all means get it made (fig. 23); but do not spend too much on it, for later on you will want a bigger and more complicated thing, which will be described in its proper place—that is to say, when we come to it; and we shall come to it when we come to deal with work made up of a number of pieces of glass, as all windows must be.

FIG. 23.

This that you have now, not being a window but a bit of glass to practise on, what I have described above will do for it.

A note to be always industrious and to work with all your might.—I advise you to put this work on an easel; but this is not the way such work is usually done;—where the work is done as a task (alas, that it could ever be so!) it is held listlessly in the left hand while touched with the right; but no artist can afford to be at this disadvantage, or at any disadvantage.

Fancy a surgeon having to hold the limb with one hand while he uses the lancet with the other, or an astronomer, while he makes his measurement, bunglingly moving his telescope by hand while he pursues his star, instead of having it driven by the clock!

You cannot afford to be less keen or less in earnest, and you want both hands free—ay! more than this—your whole body free: you must not be lazy and sit glued to your stool; you must get up and walk backwards and forwards to look at your work. Do you think art is so easy that you can afford to saunter over it?

Do, I beg you, dear reader, pay attention to these words; for it is true (though strange) that the hardest thing I have found in teaching has been to get the pupil to take the most reasonable care not to hamper and handicap himself by omitting to have his work comfortably and conveniently placed and his tools and materials in good order. You shall find a man going on painting all day, working in a messing, muddling way—wasting time and money—because his pigment has not been covered up when he left off work yesterday, and has got dusty and full of "hairs"; another will waste hour after hour, cricking his neck and squinting at his work from a corner, when thirty seconds and a little wit would move his work where he would get a good light and be comfortable; or he will work with bad tools and grumble, when five minutes would mend his tools and make him happy.

An artist's work—any artist's, but especially a glass-painter's—should be just as finished, precise, clean, and alert as a surgeon's or a dentist's. Have you not in the case of these (when the affair has not been too serious) admired the way in which the cool, white hands move about, the precision with which the finger-tips take up this or that, and when taken up use it "just *so*," neither more nor less: the spotlessness and order and perfect finish of every tool and material, from those fearsome things which (though you prefer not to dwell on their uses) you cannot help admiring, down to the snowy cotton-wool daintily poked ready through the holes in a little silver beehive? Just such skill, handling, and precision, and just such perfection of instruments, I urge as proper to painting.

What Tools are wanted to complete the Outline.—I will now describe those tools which you want at this stage, that is, *to mend your outline with.*

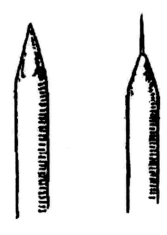

FIG. 24.

You want the brush which you used in the first instance to paint it with, and that has already been described; but you also want points of various fineness to etch it away with where it is too thick; these are the needle and the stick (fig. 24); any needle set in a handle will do, but if you want it for fine work, take care that it be sharp. "How foolish," you say; "as if you need tell us that." On the contrary,— nine people out of ten need telling, because they go upon the assumption that a needle *must* be sharp, "as sharp as a needle," and cannot need sharpening,—and they will go on for 365 days in a year wondering why a needle (which *must* be sharp) should take out so much coarser a light than they want.

Now as to "sticks"; if you make a point of soft wood it lasts for three or four touches and then gets "furred" at the point, and if of very hard wood it slips on the glass. Bamboo is good; but the best of all—that is to say for broad stick-lights—is an old, sable oil-colour brush, clogged with oil and varnish till it is as hard as horn and then cut to a point; this "clings" a little as it goes over the glass, and is most comfortable to use.

I have no doubt that other materials may be equally good, celluloid or horn, for example; the student must use his own ingenuity on such a simple matter.

How to Complete the Outline.—With the tools above described complete the outline—by adding colour with the brush where the lines are too fine, and by taking it away with needle or stick where they are too coarse; make it by these means exactly like the copy, and this is all you need do. But as an example of the degree of correctness attainable (and therefore to be demanded) are here inserted two illustrations (figs. 25 and 26), one of the example used, and the other of a copy made from it by a young apprentice.

FIG. 25.

FIG. 26.

CHAPTER IV

Matting—Badgering—How to preserve Correctness of Outline—
Difficulty of Large Work—Ill-ground Pigment—The Muller—
Overground Pigment—Taking out Lights—"Scrubs"—The Need of a
Master.

Take your camel hair matting-brush (fig. 27 or 28); fill it with the pigment, try
it on the slab of the easel till it seems just so full that the wash you put on will not
run down till you have plenty of time to brush it flat with the badger (fig. 29).

Have your badger ready at hand and *very clean*, for if there is any pigment on it
from former using, that will spoil the very delicate operation you are now to
perform.

Now rapidly, but with a very light hand, lay an even wash over the whole
piece of glass on which the outline is painted; use vertical strokes, and try to get
the touches to just meet each other without overlapping; but there is a very
important thing to observe in holding the brush. If you hold it so (fig. 30) you
cannot properly regulate the pressure, and also the pigment runs away
downwards, and the brush gets dry at the point; you must hold it so (fig. 31), then
the curve of the hair makes the brush go lightly over the surface, while also, the
body of the brush being pointed downwards, the point you are using is always
being refilled.

FIG. 27.

FIG. 28.

FIG. 29.

It takes a very skilful workman indeed to put the strokes so evenly side by side that the result looks flat and not stripy; indeed you can hardly hope to do so, but you can get rid of what "stripes" there are by taking your badger and "stabbing" the surface of the painting with it very rapidly, moving it from side to side so as never to stab twice in the same spot; this by degrees makes the colour even, by taking a little off the dark part and putting it on the light; but the result will look mottled, not flat and smooth. Sometimes this may be agreeable, it depends on what you are painting; but if you wish it to be smooth, just give a last stroke or two over the whole glass sideways, that is to say, holding the badger so that it stands quite perpendicular to the glass, move it, *always still perpendicular*, across the whole surface. You must not sway it from side to side, or kick it up at the end of each stroke like a man white-washing; it must move along so that the points of the hairs are all just lightly touching the glass all the time.

FIG. 30.

How to Ensure the Drawing of a Face being kept Correct while Painting.—If you adopt the plan of doing the first painting over an unfired outline, you must be very careful that the outline is not brushed out of drawing in the process. If you have sufficient skill it need not be so, for it is quite possible—if all the conditions as to adhesiveness are right—and if you are light-handed enough—to so lay and badger the "matt" that the outline beneath shall only be gently softened, and not blurred or moved from its place. But in any case the best plan is at the same time that you trace the outline of a head on to the glass to trace it also with equal care on to a piece of tracing paper, and arrange three or four well-marked points, such as the corner of the mouth, the pupil of the eye, and some point on the back of the head or neck, so that these cannot possibly shift, and that you may be able at any time to get the tracing back into its proper place, both on the cartoon and on the piece of glass on which you are to paint the head. On which piece of glass also your first care should be that these three or four points should be clearly marked and unmovable; then during the whole progress of the painting you will always be able to verify the correctness of the drawing by placing your piece of tracing paper over the glass, and so seeing that nothing has shifted its place.

FIG. 31.

It requires a good deal of patience and practice to lay matt successfully over unfired outline. It is a question of the amount and quality of the gum, the condition of your brush, even the dryness or dampness of the air. You must try what degree of gum suits you best, both in the outline and in the matt which you are to pass over it. Try it a good many times on a slab of plain glass or on the plate of your easel first, before you try on your painting. Of course it's a much easier thing to matt successfully over a small piece than over a large. A head as big as the palm of your hand is not a very severe test of your powers; but in one as large as the *whole* of your hand, say a head seven inches from crown to chin, the problem is increased quite immeasurably in difficulty. The real test is being able to produce in glass a real facsimile of a head by Botticelli or Holbein, and when you can do that satisfactorily you can do anything in glass-painting.

Do not aim to get *too much* in the first painting, at any rate not till you have had long practice. Be content if you get enough modelling on a head to turn the outline into a more sensitive and artistic drawing than it could be if planted down, raw and hard, upon the bare, cold glass. After all it is a common practice to fire the outline separately, and anything beyond this that you get upon the glass for first fire is so much to the good.

But besides the quality of the *gum* you will find sometimes differences in the quality or condition of the *pigment*. It may be insufficiently ground; in which case the matt, in passing over, will rasp away every vestige of the outline, so delicate a matter it is.

You can tell when colour is not ground sufficiently by the way it acts when laid as a vertical wash. Lay a wash, moist enough to "run," on a bit of your easel-slab; it will run down, making a sort of seaweed-looking pattern—clear lanes of light on the glass with a black grain at the lower end. Those are the bits of unground material: under a 100-diameter microscope they look like chunks of ironstone or road metal, or of rusty iron, and you'll soon understand why they have scratched away your tender outline.

You must grind such colour till it is smooth, and an old-fashioned *granite* muller is the thing, not a glass one.

Now, after all this, how am I to excuse the paradox that it is possible to have the colour ground *too* fine! All one can say is that you "find it so." It can be so fine that it seems to slip about in a thin, oily kind of way.

It's all as you find it; the differences of a craft are endless; there is no forecasting of everything, and you must buy your experience, like everybody else, and find what suits you, learning your skill and your materials side by side.

Now these are the chief processes of painting, as far as laying on colour goes; but you still have much of your work before you, for the way in which light and shade is got on glass is almost more in "taking off" than in "putting on." You have laid your dark "matt" all over the glass evenly; now the next thing is to remove it wherever you want light or half-tone.

FIG. 32.

How to Finish a Shaded Painting out of the Even Matt.—This is done in many ways, but chiefly with those tools which painters call "scrubs," which are oil-colour hog-hair brushes, either worn down by use, or rubbed down on fine sandpaper till they are as stiff as you like them to be. You want them different in this: some harder, some softer; some round, some square, and of various sizes (figs. 32 and 33), and with these you brush the matt away gently and by degrees, and so make a light and shade drawing of it. It is exactly like the process of mezzotint, where, after a surface like that of a file has been laboriously produced over the whole copper-plate, the engraver removes it in various degrees, leaving the original to stand entirely only for the darkest of all shadows, and removing it all entirely only in the highest lights.

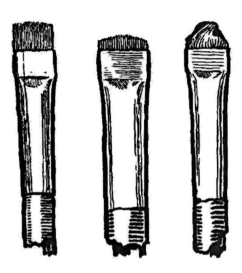

FIG. 33.

There is nothing for this but practice; there is nothing more to *tell* about it; as the conjurers say, "That's how it's done." You will find difficulties, and as these occur you will think this a most defective book. "Why on earth," you will say, "didn't he tell us about this, about that, about the other?" Ah, yes! it is a most defective book; if it were not, I would have taken good care not to write it. For the worst thing that could happen to you would be to suppose that any book can possibly teach you any craft, and take the place of a master on the one hand, and of years of practice on the other.

This book is not intended to do so; it is written to give as much information and to arouse as much interest as a book can; with the hope that if any are in a position to wish to learn this craft, and have not been brought up to it, they may learn, in general, what its conditions are, and then be able to decide whether to carry it further by seeking good teaching, and by laying themselves out for a patient course of study and practice and many failures and experiments. While, with regard to those already engaged in glass-painting, it is of course intended to arouse their interest in, and to give them information upon, those other branches of their craft which are not generally taught to those brought up as glass-painters.

CHAPTER V

Cutting (advanced)—The Ideal Cartoon—The Cut-line—Setting the
Cartoon—Transferring the Cut-line to the Glass—Another Way—Some
Principles of Taste—Countercharging.

We have only as yet spoken of the processes of cutting and painting in
themselves, and as they can be practised on a single bit of glass; but now we must
consider them as applied to a subject in glass where many pieces must be used.
This is a different matter indeed, and brings in all the questions of taste and
judgment which make the difference between a good window and an inferior one.
Now, first, you must know that every differently coloured piece must be cut out
by itself, and therefore must have a strip of lead round it to join it to the others.

Draw a cartoon of a figure, *bearing this well in mind*: you must draw it in such a
simple and severe way that you do not set impossible or needlessly difficult tasks
to the cutter. Look now, for example, at the picture in Plate V. by Mr. Selwyn
Image—how simple the cutting!

You think it, perhaps, too "severe"? You do not like to see the leads so
plainly. You would like better something more after the "Munich" school, where
the lead line is disguised or circumvented. If so, my lesson has gone wrong; but
we must try and get it right.

You would like it better because it is "more of a picture"; exactly, but you
ought to like the other better because it is "more of a window." Yes, even if all
else were equal, you ought to like it better, *because* the lead lines cut it up. Keep
your pictures for the walls and your windows for the holes in them.

But all else is *not* equal: and, supposing you now standing before a window of
the kind I speak of, I will tell you what has been sacrificed to get this "picture-
window" "like a picture." *Stained-glass* has been sacrificed; for this is *not* stained-
glass, it is painted glass—that is to say, it is coloured glass ground up into
powders and painted on to white sheets of glass: a poor, miserable substitute for
the glorious colour of the deep amethyst and ruby-coloured glasses which it
pretends to ape. You will not be in much danger of using it when you have
handled your stained-glass samples for a while and learned to love them. You will
love them so much that you will even get to like the severe lead line which
announces them for what they are.

But you must get to reasonably love it as a craft limitation, a necessity, a thing
which places bounds and limits to what you can do in this art, and prevents
tempting and specious tricks.

How to Make a "Cut-line."—But now, all this being granted, how are we to set
about getting the pieces cut? First of all, I would say that it is always well to draw
most, if not all, of the necessary lead lines on the cartoon itself. By the necessary
lead lines I mean those which separate different colours; for you know that there
must be a lead line between these. Then, when these are drawn, it is a question of
convenience whether to draw in also the more or less optional lead lines which

break up each space of uniform colour into convenient-sized pieces. If you do not want your cartoon afterwards for any other purpose you may as well do so: that is, first "set" the cartoon if it is in charcoal or chalk, and then try the places for these lead lines lightly in charcoal over the drawing: working thus, you can dust them away time after time till they seem right to you, and then either set them also or not as you choose.

A good, useful setting-mixture for large quantities is composed by mixing equal parts of "white polish" and methylated spirit; allowing it to settle for a week, and pouring off all that is clear. It is used in the ordinary way with a spray diffuser, and will keep for any length of time.

The next step is to make what is called the cut-line. To do this, pin a piece of tracing-cloth over the whole cartoon; this can be got from any artist's-colourman or large stationer. Pin it over the cartoon with the dull surface outwards, and with a soft piece of charcoal draw lines 1/16 to 1/8 of an inch wide down the centre of all the lead lines: remove the cloth from the cartoon, and if any of the lines look awkward or ugly, now that you see them by themselves undisguised by the drawing below, alter them, and then, finally, with a long, thin brush paint them in, over the charcoal, with water-colour lamp-black, this time a true sixteenth of an inch wide. Don't dust the charcoal off first, it makes the paint cling much better to the shiny cloth.

When this is done, there is a choice of three ways for cutting the glass. One is to make shaped pieces of cartridge-paper as patterns to cut each bit of glass by; another is to place the bits of glass, one by one, over the cut-line and cut freehand by the line you see through the glass. This latter process needs no description, but you cannot employ it for dark glasses because you cannot see the line through: for this you must employ one of the other methods.

How to Transfer the Cutting-line on to the Glass.—Take a bit of glass large enough to cut the piece you want; place it, face upwards, on the table; place the cut-line over it in its proper place, and then slip between them, without moving either, a piece of black "transfer paper": then, with a style or hard pencil, trace the cutting-line down on to the glass. This will not make a black mark visible on the glass, it will only make a *grease* mark, and that hardly visible, not enough to cut by; but take a soft dabber—a lump of cotton-wool tied up in a bit of old handkerchief—and with this, dipped in dry whitening or powdered white chalk, dab the glass all over; then blow the surface and you will see a clear white line where the whitening has stuck to the greasy line made by the transfer paper; and by this you can cut very comfortably.

But a third way is to cut the shape of each piece of glass out in cartridge-paper; and to do this you put the cut-line down over a sheet of "continuous-cartridge" or "cartoon" paper, as it is called, and press along all the lines with a style or hard pencil, so as to make a furrow on the paper beneath; then, after removing the cut-line, you place a sheet of ordinary window-glass below the paper and cut out each piece, between the "furrows" leaving a *full* 1/16 of an inch.

This sixteenth of an inch represents the "heart" or core of the future *lead*; it is the distance which the actual bits of glass lie one from the other in the window. You must use a very sharp penknife, and you will find that, cutting against *glass*, each shape will have quite a smooth edge; and round this you can cut with your diamond.

This method, which is far the most accurate and craftsmanly way of cutting glass, is best used with the actual diamond: in that case you feel the edge of the paper all the time with the diamond-spark; but in cutting with the wheel you must not rest against the edge of the paper; otherwise you will be sure to cut into it. Now, whichever of all these processes you employ, remember that there must be a *full* 1/16 of an inch left between each piece of glass and all its neighbours.

The reason why you leave this space between the pieces is that the core of the lead is about that or a little less in thickness: the closer the glass fits to this the better, but no part of the glass must go *nearer* to its neighbour than this, otherwise the work will be pressed outwards, and you will not be able to get the whole of the panel within its proper limits.

FIG. 34.

Fig. 34 is an illustration of various kinds and sizes of lead; showing some with the glass inserted in its place. By all means make your leads yourself, for many of those ready made are not lead at all, or not pure lead. Get the parings of sheet lead from a source you can trust, and cast them roughly in moulds as at fig. 35. Fig. 36 is the shears by which the strips may be cut; fig. 37 is the lead-mill or "vice" by which they are milled and run into their final shape; fig. 38 the "cheeks" or blocks through which the lead passes. The working of such an instrument is a thing that is understood in a few minutes with the instrument itself at hand, but it is cumbrous to explain in writing, and not worth while; since if you purchase such a thing, obviously the seller will be there to explain its use. Briefly,—the handle turns two wheels with milled edges 1/16 of an inch apart; which, at one motion, draw the lead between them, mill it, and force it between the two "cheeks" (fig. 38), which mould the outside of the lead in its passage. These combined movements, by a continuous pressure, squeeze out the strip of lead into about twice its length; correspondingly decreasing its thickness and finishing it as it goes.

FIG. 35.

FIG. 36.

Fig. 37.

Some principles of good taste and common sense with regard to the cutting up of a Window; according to which the Cartoon and Design must be modified.—Never disguise the lead line. Cut the necessary parts first, as I said before; cut the optional parts *simply*; thinking most of craft-convenience, and not much of realism.

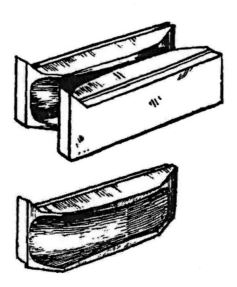

FIG. 38.

Do not, however, go to the extent of making two lead lines cross each other. Fig. 39 shows the two kinds of joint, A being the wrong one (as I hold), and B the right one; but, after all, this is partly a question of taste.

Do not cut borders and other minor details into measured spaces; cut them hap-hazard.

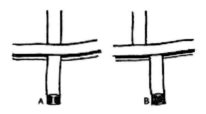

FIG. 39.

Do not cut leafage too much by the outlines of the groups of leaves—or wings by the outlines of the groups of feathers.

Do not outline with lead lines any forms of minor importance.

Do not allow the whole of any figure to cut out dark against light, or light against dark; but if the figure is ever so bright, let an inch or two of its outline tell out as a dark against a spot of still brighter light; and if it is ever so dark, be it red or blue as strong as may be, let an inch or two of its outline tell out against a still stronger dark in the background, if you have to paint it pitch-black to do so.

By this "countercharging" (as heralds say), your composition will melt together with a pleasing mystery; for you must always remember that a window is, after all, only a window, it is not the church, and nothing in it should stare out at you so that you cannot get away from it; windows should "dream," and should be so treated as to look like what they are, the apertures to admit the light; subjects painted on a thin and brittle film, hung in mid-air between the light and the dark.

CHAPTER VI

Painting (advanced)—Waxing-up—Cleanliness—Further Methods of Painting—Stipple—Dry Stipple—Film—Effects of Distance—Danger of Over-Painting—Frying.

I have mentioned all these points of judgment and good taste we have just finished speaking of, because they are matters that must necessarily come before you at the time you are making the cartoon, the preliminary drawing of the window, and before you come to handle the glass at all.

But it is now necessary to tell you how the whole of the glass, when it is cut, must be fixed together, so that you can both see it and paint upon it as a whole picture. This is done as follows:—

First place the cut-line (for the making of which you have already had instructions) face upwards on the bench, and over it place a sheet of glass, as large at least as the piece you mean to paint. Thick window-glass, what glass-makers call "thirty-two ounce sheet"—that is, glass that weighs about thirty-two ounces to the square foot—will do well enough for very small subjects, but for anything over a few square feet, it is better to use thin plate-glass. This is expensive, but you do not want the best; what is called "patent plate" does quite well, and cheap plate-glass can often be got to suit you at the salvage stores, whither it is brought from fires.

Having laid your sheet of glass down upon the cut-line, place upon it all the bits of glass in their proper places; then take beeswax (and by all means let it be the best and purest you can get; get it at a chemist's, not at the oil-shop), and heat a few ounces of it in a saucepan, and *when all of it is melted*—not before, and as little after as may be—take any convenient tool, a penknife or a strip of glass, and, dipping it rapidly into the melted wax, convey it in little drops to the points where the various bits of glass meet each other, dropping a single drop of wax at each joint. It is no advantage to have any extra drops along the *sides* of the bits; if each *corner* is properly secured, that is all that is needed (fig. 40).

Some people use a little resin or tar with the wax to make it more brittle, so that when the painting is finished and the work is to be taken down again off the plate, the spots of wax will chip off more easily. I do not advise it. Boys in the shop who are just entering their apprenticeship get very skilful, and quite properly so, in doing this work; waxing up yard after yard of glass, and never dropping a spot of wax on the surface.

It is much to be commended: all things done in the arts should be done as well as they can be done, if only for the sake of character and training; but in this case it is a positive advantage that the work should be done thus cleanly, because if a spot of wax is dropped on the surface of the glass that is to be painted on, the spot must be carefully scraped off and every vestige of it removed with a wet duster dipped in a little grit of some kind—pigment does well—otherwise the glass is greasy and the painting will not adhere.

FIG. 40.

For the same reason the wax-saucepan should be kept very clean, and the wax frequently poured off, and all sediment thrown away. A bit of cotton-fluff off the duster is enough to drag a "lump" out on the end of the waxing-tool, which, before you have time to notice it, will be dribbling over the glass and perhaps spoiling it; for you must note that sometimes it is necessary to re-wax down *unfired* work, which a drop of wax the size of a pinhole, flirted off from the end of the tool, will utterly ruin. How important, then, to be cleanly.

And in this matter of removing such spots from *fired* work, do please note that you should *use the knife and the duster alternately* for *each spot*. Do not scrape a batch of the spots off first and then go over the ground again with the duster—this can only save a second or two of time, and the merest fraction of trouble; and these are ill saved indeed at the cost of doing the work ill. And you are sure to do it so, for when the spot is scraped off it is very difficult to see where it was; you are sure to miss some, in going over the glass with a duster, and you will discover them again, to your cost and annoyance, when you matt over them for the second painting: and, just when you cannot afford to spare a single moment—in some critical process—they will come out like round o's in the middle of your shading, compelling you to break off your work and do now what should have been done before you began to paint.

But the best plan of all is to avoid the whole thing by doing the work cleanly from the first. And it is quite easy; for all you have to do is to carry the tool horizontally till it is over the spot where you want the wax, and then, by a tilt of the hand, slide the drop into its place.

Further Methods of Painting.—There are two chief methods of treating the matt—one is the "stipple," and the other the "film" or badgered matt.

The Stipple.—When you have put on your matt with the camel-hair brush, take a stippling brush (fig. 41) and stab the matt all over with it while it is wet. A great variety of texture can be got in this way, for you may leave off the process at any moment; if you leave it off soon, the work will be soft and blurred, for, not being dry, the pigment will spread again as soon as you leave off: but, if you choose, you can go on stippling till the whole is dry, when the pigment will gather up into little sharp spots like pepper, and the glass between them will be almost clear. You must bear in mind that you cannot use scrubs over work like the last described, and cannot use them to much advantage over stipple at all. You can draw a needle through; but as a rule you do not want to take lights out of stipple, since you can complete the shading in the single process by stippling more or less according to the light and shade you want.

FIG. 41.

A very coarse form of the process is "dry" stippling, where you stipple straight on to the surface of the clear glass, with pigment taken up off the palette by the stippling brush itself: for coarse distant work this may be sometimes useful.

Now as to film. We have spoken of laying on an even matt and badgering it smooth; and you can use this with a certain amount of stipple also with very good effect; but you are to notice one great rule about these two processes, namely, that the same amount of pigment *obscures much more light used in film than used in stipple.*

Light *spreads* as it comes through openings; and a very little light let, in pinholes, through a very dark matt, will, at a distance, so assert itself as to prevail over the darkness of the matt.

It is really very little use going on to describe the way the colour acts in these various processes; for its behaviour varies with every degree of all of them. One may gradually acquire the skill to combine all the processes, in all their degrees, upon a single painting; and the only way in which you can test their relative value, either as texture or as light and shade, is to constantly practise each process in all its degrees, and see what results each has, both when seen near at hand and also when seen from a distance. It is useless to try and learn these things from written directions; you must make them your own, as precious secrets, by much practice and much experiment, though it will save you years of both to learn under a good master.

But this question of distance is a most important thing, and we must enlarge upon it a little and try to make it quite clear.

Glass-painting is not like any other painting in this respect.

Let us say that you see an oil-painting—a portrait—at the end of the large room in some big Exhibition. You stand near it and say, "Yes, that is the King" (or the Commander-in-Chief), "a good likeness; however do they do those patent-leather boots?" But after you have been down one side of the room and turn round at the other end to yawn, you catch sight of it again; and still you say, "Yes, it's a good likeness," and "really those boots are very clever!" But if it had been your own painting on *glass*, and sitting at your easel you had at last said, "Yes,— now it's like the drawing—*that's* the expression," you could by no means safely count on being able to say the same at all distances. You may say it at ten feet off, at twenty, and yet at thirty the shades may all gather together into black patches; the drawing of the eyelids and eyes may vanish in one general black blot, the half-tones on the cheeks may all go to nothing. These actual things, for instance, *will* be the result if the cheeks are stippled or scrubbed, and the shade round the eyes left as a *film*—ever so slight a film will do it. Seen near, you *see the drawing through the film*; but as you go away the light will come pouring stronger and stronger through the brush or stipple marks on the cheeks, until all films will cut out against it like black spots, altering the whole expression past recognition.

Try this on simple terms:—

Do a face on white glass in strong outline only: step back, and the face goes to nothing; strengthen the outline till the forms are quite monstrous—the outline of the nose as broad as the bridge of it—still, at a given distance, it goes to nothing; the expression varies every step back you take. But now, take a matting brush, with a film so thin that it is hardly more than dirty water; put it on the back of the glass (so as not to wash up your outline); badger it flat, so as just to dim the glass less than "ground glass" is dimmed;—and you will find your outline look almost the same at each distance. It is the pure light that plays tricks, and it will play them through a pinhole.

And now, finally, let us say that you may do anything you *can* do in the painting of glass, so long as you do not lay the colour on too thick. The outline-touches should be flat upon the glass, and above all things should not be laid on so wet, or laid on so thick, that the pigment forms into a "drop" at the end of the touch; for this drop, and all pigment that is thick upon the glass like that, will "fry" when it is put into the kiln: that is to say, being so thick, and standing so far from the surface of the glass, it will fire separately from the glass itself and stand as a separate crust above it, and this will perish.

Plate IX. shows the appearance of the bubbles or blisters in a bit of work that has fried, as seen under a microscope of 20 diameters; and if you are inclined to disregard the danger of this defect as seen of its natural size, when it is a mere roughness on the glass, what do you think of it *now*? You can remove it at once by scraping it with a knife; and indeed, if through accident a touch here and there does fry, it is your only plan to so remove it. All you can scrape off should be scraped off and repainted every time the glass comes from the kiln; and that brings us to the important question of *firing*.

CHAPTER VII

Firing—Three Kinds of Kiln—Advantages and Disadvantages—The Gas-Kiln—Quick Firing—Danger—Sufficient Firing—Soft Pigments—Difference in Glasses—"Stale" Work—The Scientific Facts—How to Judge of Firing—Drawing the Kiln.

The way in which the painting is attached to the glass and made permanent is by firing it in a kiln at great heat, and thus fusing the two together.

Simple enough to say, but who is to describe in writing this process in all its forms? For there is, perhaps, nothing in the art of stained-glass on which there is greater diversity of opinion and diversity of practice than this matter of firing. But let us make a beginning by saying that there are, it may be said, three chief modifications of the process.

First, the use of the old, closed, coke or turf kiln.

Second, of the closed gas-kiln.

And third, of the open gas-kiln.

The first consists of a chamber of brick or terra-cotta, in which the glass is placed on a bed of powdered whitening, on iron plates, one above another like shelves, and the whole enclosed in a chamber where the heat is raised by a fire of coke or peat.

This, be it understood, is a slow method. The heat increases gradually, and applies to the glass what the kiln-man calls a "good, soaking heat." The meaning of this expression, of course, is that the gradual heat gives time for the glass and the pigment to fuse together in a natural way, more likely to be good and permanent in its results than a process which takes a twentieth part of the time and which therefore (it is assumed) must wrench the materials more harshly from their nature and state.

There are, it must be admitted, one or two things to be said for this view which require answering.

First, that this form of kiln has the virtue of being old; for in such a thing as this, beyond all manner of doubt, was fired all the splendid stained-glass of the Middle Ages.

Second, that by its use one is entirely preserved from the dangers attached to the *misuse* of the gas-kiln.

But the answers to these two things are—

First, that the method employed in the Middle Ages did not invariably ensure permanence. Any one who has studied stained-glass must be familiar with cases in which ancient work has faded or perished.

The second claim is answered by the fact, I think beyond dispute, that all objections to the use of the gas-kiln would be removed if it were used properly; it is not the use of it as a process which is in itself dangerous, but merely the misuse of it. People must be content with what is reasonable in the matter; and, knowing that the gas-kiln is spoken of as the "quick-firing" kiln, they must not insist on trying to fire *too* quick.

Now I have the highest authority (that of the makers of both kiln and pigment) to support my own conviction, founded on my own experience, in what I am here going to say.

Observe, then, that up to the point at which actual fusion commences—that is, when pigment and glass begin to get soft—there is no advantage in slowness, and therefore none in the use of fuel as against gas—no possible *disadvantage* as far as the work goes: only it is time wasted. But where people go wrong is in not observing the vital importance of proceeding gently when fusion *does* commence. For in the actual process of firing, when fusion is about to commence, it is indeed all-important to proceed gently; otherwise the work will "fry," and, in fact, it is in danger from a variety of causes. Make it, then, your practice to aim at twenty to twenty-five minutes, instead of ten or twelve, as the period during which the pigment is to be fired, and regulate the amount of heat you apply by that standard. The longer period of moderate heat means safety. The shorter period of great heat means danger, and rather more than danger.

Fig. 42 is the closed gas-kiln, where the glass is placed in an enclosed chamber; fig. 43 is the open gas-kiln, where the gas plays on the roof of the chamber in which the glass lies; fig. 44 shows this latter. But no written description or picture is really sufficient to make it safe for you to use these gas-kilns. You would be sure to have some serious accident, probably an explosion; and as it is absolutely necessary for you to have instruction, either from the maker or the experienced user of them, it is useless for me to tell lamely what they could show thoroughly. I shall therefore leave this essentially technical part of the subject, and, omitting these details, speak of the few *principles* which regulate the firing of glass.

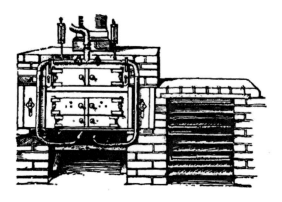

FIG. 42.

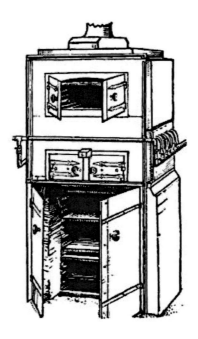

FIG. 43.

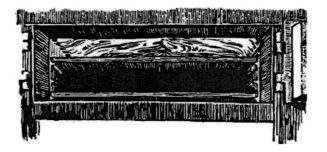

FIG. 44.

And the first is to *fire it enough*. Whatever pigment you use, and with whatever flux, none will be permanent if the work is under-fired; indeed I believe that under-firing is far more the cause of stained-glass perishing than the use of untrustworthy pigment or flux; although it must always be borne in mind that the use of a soft pigment, which will "fire beautifully" at a low heat, with a fine gloss on the surface, is always to be avoided. The pigment is fused, no doubt; but is it united to the glass? What one would like to have would be a pigment whose own fusing-point was the same, or about the same, as that of the glass itself, so that the surface, at least, of the piece of glass softens to receive it and lets it right down into itself. You should never be satisfied with the firing of your glass unless it presents two qualifications: first, that the surface of the glass has melted and begun to run together; and second, that the fused pigment is quite glossy and shiny, not the least dull or rusty looking, when the glass is cool.

"What one would like to have."

And can you not get it?

Well, yes! but you want experience and constant watchfulness—in short, "rule of thumb." For every different glass differs in hardness, and you never know, except by memory and constant handling of the stuff, exactly what your materials are going to do in the kiln; for as to standardising, so as to get the glass into any known relation with the pigment in the matter of fusing, the thing has never, as far as I know, been attempted. It probably could not be done with regard to all, or even many, glasses—nor need it; though perhaps it might be well if a nearer approach to it could be achieved with regard to the manufacture of the lighter tinted glasses, the "whites" especially, on which the heads and hands are painted, and where consequently it is of such vital importance that the painting should have careful justice done to it, and not lose in the firing through uncertainty with regard to conditions.

Nevertheless, if you observe the rule to fire sufficiently, the worst that can happen is a disappointment to yourself from the painting having to an unnecessary extent "fired away" in the kiln. You must be patient, and give it a second painting; and as to the "rule of thumb," it is surprising how one gets to know, by constant handling the stuff, how the various glasses are going to behave in the fire. It was the method of the Middle Ages which we are so apt to praise, and there is much to be said for practical, craftsmanly experience, especially in the arts, as against a system of formulas based on scientific knowledge. It would be a pity indeed to get rid of the accidental and all the delight which it brings, and we must take it with its good and bad.

The second rule with regard to the question of firing is to take care that the work is not "stale" when it goes into the kiln. Every one will tell you a different tale about many points connected with glass, just as doctors disagree in every affair of life. In talking over this matter of keeping the colour fresh—even talking it over with one's practical and experienced friends generally—one will sometimes hear the remark that "they don't see that delay can do it much harm;" and when one asks, "Can it do it any good?" the reply will be, "Well, probably it would be as well to fire it soon;" or in the case of mixing, "To use it fresh." Now, if it would be "as well"—which really means "on the safe side"—then that seems a sufficient reason for any reasonable man.

But indeed I have always found it one of the chiefest difficulties with pupils to get them to take the most reasonable precautions to *make quite sure* of *anything*. It is just the same with matters of measurement, although upon these such vital issues depend. How weary one gets of the phrase "it's not far out"—the obvious comment of a reasonable man upon such a remark, of course, being that if it is out *at all* it's, at any rate, *too* far out. A French assistant that I had once used always to complain of my demanding (as he expressed it) such "rigorous accuracy." But there are only two ways—to be accurate or inaccurate; and if the former is possible, there is no excuse for the latter.

But as to this question of freshness of colour, which is of such paramount importance, I may quote the same authority I used before—that of the *maker of the colour*—to back my own experience and previous conviction on the point, which certainly is that fresh colour, used the same day it is ground and fired the same day it is used, fires better and fires away less than any other.

The facts of the case, scientifically, I am assured, are as follows. The pigment contains a large amount of soft glass in a very fine state of division, and the carbonic acid, which all air contains (especially that of workshops), will immediately begin to enter into combination with the alkalis of the glass, throw out the silica, and thus disintegrate what was brought together in the first instance when the glass was made. The result of this is that this intruder (the carbonic acid) has to be driven out again by the heat of the kiln, and is quite likely to disturb the pigment in every possible way in the process of its escape. I have myself sometimes noticed, when some painted work has been laid aside unusually long before firing, some white efflorescence or crystallisation taking place and coming out as a white dust on the painted surface.

Now it is not necessary to know here, in a scientific or chemical sense, what has actually taken place. Two things are evident to common sense. One, that the change is organic, and the other that it is unpremeditated; and therefore, on both grounds, it is a thing to avoid, which indeed my friend's scientific explanation sufficiently confirms. It is well, therefore, on all accounts to paint swiftly and continuously, and to fire as soon as you can; and above all things not to let the colour lie about getting stale on the palette. Mix no more for the day than you mean to use; clean your palette every day or nearly so; work up all the colour each time you set your palette, and do not give way to that slovenly and idle practice that is sometimes seen, of leaving a crust of dry colour to collect, perhaps for days or weeks, round the edge of the mass on your palette, and then some day, when the spirit moves you, working this in with the rest, to imperil the safety of your painting.

How to Know when the Glass is Fired Sufficiently.—This is told by the colour as it lies in the kiln—that is, in such a kiln that you can see the glass; but who can describe a colour? You have nothing for this but to buy your experience. But in kilns that are constructed with a peephole, you can also tell by putting in a bright iron rod or other shining object and holding it over the glass so as to see if the glass reflects it. If the pigment is raw it will (if there is enough of it on the glass to cover the surface) prevent the piece of glass from reflecting the rod; but directly it is fired the pigment itself becomes glossy, and then the surface will reflect.

This is all a matter of practice; nothing can describe the "look" of a piece of glass that is fired. You must either watch batch after batch for yourself and learn by experience, or get a good kiln-man to point out fired and unfired, and call your attention to the slight shades of colour and glow which distinguish one from the other.

On Taking the Glass out of the Fire.—And so you take the glass out of the fire. In the old kilns you take the fire away from the glass, and leave the glass to cool all night or so; in the new, you remove it and leave it in moderate heat at the side of the kiln till it is cool enough to handle, or nearly cold. And then you hold it up and look at it.

CHAPTER VIII

The Second Painting—Disappointment with Fired Work—A False
Remedy—A Useful Tool—The Needle—A Resource of Desperation—
The Middle Course—Use of the Finger—The Second Painting—
Procedure.

And when you have looked at it, as I said just now you should do, your first
thought will be a wish that you had never been born. For no one, I suppose, ever
took his first batch of painted glass out of the kiln without disappointment and
without wondering what use there is in such an art. For the painting when it went
in was grey, and silvery, and sharp, and crisp, and firm, and brilliant. Now all is
altered; all the relations of light and shade are altered; the sharpness of every
brush-mark is gone, and everything is not only "washed out" to half its depth, but
blurred at that. Even if you could get it, by a second painting, to look exactly as it
was at first, you think: "What a waste of life! I thought I had done! It was *right* as
it was; I was pleased so far; but now I am tired of the thing; I don't want to be
doing it all over again."

Well, my dear reader, I cannot tell you a remedy for this state of things—it is
one of the conditions of the craft; you must find by experience what pigment, and
what glass, and what style of using them, and what amount of fire give the least of
these disappointing results, and then make the best of it; and make up your mind
to do without certain effects in glass, which you find are unattainable.

There is, however, one remedy which I suppose all glass-painters try, but
eventually discard. I suppose we have all passed through the stage of working very
dark, to allow for the firing-off; and I want to say a word of warning which may
prevent many heartaches in this matter. I having passed through them all, there is
no reason why others should. Now mark very carefully what follows, for it is
difficult to explain, and you cannot afford to let the sense slip by you.

I told you that a film left untouched would always come out as a black patch
against work that was pierced with the scrub, however slightly.

Now, herein lies the difficulty of working with a very thick matt; for if it is
thick enough on the cheek and brow of a face to give strong modelling when
fired, *then whenever it has passed over the previous outline-painting, for example, in the eyes,
mouth, nostrils, &c., you will find that the two together have become too thick for the scrub to
move.*

Now you do not need, as an artist, to be told that it is fatal to allow *any* part of
your painting to be thus beyond your control; to be obliged to say, "It's too dark,
but unfortunately I have no tools that will lighten it—it will not yield to the
scrub."

However, a certain amount can be done in this direction by using, on the
shadows that are *just* too strong for the scrub, a tool made by grinding down on
sandpaper a large hog-hair brush, and, of these, what are called stencil-brushes are
as good as any (fig. 45).

You do not use this by dragging it over the glass as you drag a scrub, but by *pricking* the whole of the surface which you wish to lighten. This will make little pinholes all over it, which will be sufficient to let the patch of shadow gently down to the level of the surrounding lighter modelling, and will prevent your dark shadows looking like actual "patches," as we described them doing a little way back.

FIG. 45.

Further than this you cannot go: for I cannot at all see how the next process I am to describe can be a good one, though I once thought, as I suppose most do, that it would really solve the difficulty. What I allude to is the use of the needle.

Of Work Etched out with a Needle.—The needle is a very good and useful tool for stained glass, in certain operations, but I am now to speak of it as being used over whole areas *as a substitute for the scrub, in order to deal with a matt too dense for the scrub to penetrate.*

The needle will, to be sure, remove such a matt; that is to say, will remove lines out of it, quite clear and sharp, and this, too, out of a matt so dense, that what remains does not fire away much in the kiln. Here is a tempting thing then! to have one's work unchanged by the fire! And if you could achieve this without changing the character of the work for the worse, no doubt this method would be a very fine thing. But let me trace it step by step and try to describe what happens.

You have painted your outline and you put a very heavy matt over it.

Peril No. 1.—If your matt is so dense that it will not *fire off*, it must very nearly approach the point of density at which it will *fry*. How then about the portions of it which have been painted on, as I have said, over *another* layer of pigment in the shape of the *outline*? Here is a *danger*. But even supposing that all is safe, and that you have just stopped short of the danger point. You have now your dense, rich, brown matt, with the outline just showing through it. Proceed to model it with the needle. The first stroke will really frighten you; for a flash of silver light will spring along after the point of the needle, so dazzling in contrast to the extreme dark of the matt that it looks as if the plate had been cut in two, while the matt beside it becomes pitch-black by contrast. Well, you go on, and by putting more strokes, and reducing the surrounding darkness generally, you get the drawing to look grey—but you get it to look like a grey *pen-drawing* or *etching*, not like a painting at all. We will suppose that this seems to you no disadvantage (though I must say, at once, that I think it a very great one); but now you come to the deep shadows; and these, I need hardly say, cut themselves out, more than ever, like dark patches or blots, in the manner already spoken of. You try pricking it with the brush I have described for that operation, and it will not do it; then you resort to the needle itself, and you are startled at the little, hard, glittering specks that come jumping out of the black shadow at each touch. You get a finer needle, and then you sharpen even that on the hone; and perhaps then, by pricking gingerly round the edges of the shadows, you may get the drawing and modelling to melt together fairly well. But beware! for if there is one dot of light too many, the expression of the head goes to the winds. Let us say that such a thing occurs; you have pricked one pinhole too many round the corner of the mouth.

What can you do?

You take your tracing-brush and try to mend it with a touch of pigment; and so on, and so on; till you timidly say (feeling as if you had been walking among egg-shells for the last hour), "Well, I *think* it will *do*, and I daren't touch it any more." And supposing by these means you get a head that looks really what you wanted; the work is all what glass-painters call "rotten"; liable to flake off at the least touch; isolated bits of thick crust, cut sheer out from each other, with clear glass between.

In short, the thing is a niggling and botching sort of process to my mind, and I hope that the above description is sufficiently life-like to show that I have really given it a good trial myself—with, as a result, the conclusion certainly strongly borne home to me, that the delight of having one's work unchanged by the fire is too dearly purchased at the cost of it.

How to get the greatest degree of Strength into your Painting without Danger.—Short of using a needle then, and a matt that will only yield to that instrument, I would advise, if you want the work strong, that you should paint the matt so that it will just yield, and only just, and that with difficulty, to the scrub; and, before you use this tool, just pass the finger, lightly, backwards and forwards over the matted surface. This will take out a shimmer of light here and there, according to the inequalities of the texture in the glass itself; the first touches of the scrub will not then look so startling and hard as if taken out of the dead, even matt; and also this rubbing of the finger across the surface seems to make the matt yield more easily to the tool. The dust remaining on the surface perhaps helps this; anyhow, this is as far as you can go on the side of strength in the work. You can of course "back" the work, that is, paint on the back as well as the front—a mere film at the back; but this is a method of a rather doubtful nature. The pigment on the back does not fire equally well with that on the front, and when the window is in its place, that side will be, you must bear in mind, exposed to the weather.

I have spoken incidentally of rubbing the glass with the finger as a part of painting; but the practice can be carried further and used more generally than I have yet said: the little "pits" and markings on the surface of the glass, which I mentioned when I spoke of the "right and wrong sides" of the material, can be drawn into the service of the window sometimes with very happy effect. Being treated with matt and then rubbed with the finger, they often produce very charming varieties of texture on the glass, which the painter will find many ways of making useful.

Of the Second Painting of Glass after it has been Fired.—So far we have only spoken of the appearance of work after its first fire, and its influence upon choice of method for *first painting*; but there is of course the resource which is the proper subject of this chapter, namely, the second painting.

Very small work can be done with one fire; but only very skilful painters can get work, on any large scale, strong enough for one fire to serve, and that only with the use of backing. Of course if very faint tones of shadow satisfy you, the work can be done with one fire; but if it is well fired it must almost of necessity be pale. Some people like it so—it is a matter of taste, and there can be no pronouncement made about it; but if you wish your work to look strong in light and shade—stronger than one painting will make it—I advise you, when the work comes back from the fire and is waxed up for the second time (which, in any case, it assuredly should be, if only for your judgment upon it), to proceed as follows.

First, with a tracing-brush, go over all the lines and outlined shadows that seem too weak, and then, when these touches are quite dry, pass a thin matt over the whole, and with stippling-brushes of various sizes, stipple it nearly all away while wet. You will only have about five minutes in which to deal with any one piece of glass in this way, and in the case of a head, for example, it needs a skilful hand to complete it in that short space of time. The best plan is to make several "shots" at it; if you do not hit the mark the first time, you may the second or the third. I said "stipple it nearly all away"; but the amount left must be a matter of taste; nevertheless, you must note that if you do not remove enough to make the work look "silvery," it is in danger of looking "muddy." All the ordinary resources of the painter's art may be brought in here: retouching into the half-dry second matt, dabbing with the finger—in short, all that might be done if the thing were a water-colour or an oil-painting; but it is quite useless to attempt to describe these deftnesses of hand in words: you may use any and every method of modifying the light and shade that occurs to you.

CHAPTER IX

Of Staining and Aciding—Yellow Stain—Aciding—Caution required in
Use—Remedy for Burning—Uses of Aciding—Other Resources of
Stained-Glass Work.

Yellow stain, or silver stain as some call it, is made in various ways from
silver—chloride, sulphate, and nitrate, I understand, are all used. The stain is laid
on exactly like the pigment, but at the back of the glass. It does not work very
smoothly, and some painters like to mix it with Venice turpentine instead of water
to get rid of this defect; whichever you use, keep a separate set of tools and a
separate palette for it, and always keep them clean and the stain fresh mixed. Also
you should not fire it with so strong a heat, and therefore, of course, you should
never fire pigment and stain in the same batch in the kiln; otherwise the stain will
probably go much hotter in colour than you wish, or will get muddy, or will
"metal" as painters call it—that is, get a horny, burnt-sienna look instead of a clear
yellow.

How to Etch the Flash off a Flashed Glass with Acid.—There is only one more
process, having to do with painting, which I shall describe, and that is "aciding."
By this process you can etch the flash off the flashed glasses where you like. The
process is the same as etching—you "stop-out" the parts that you wish to remain,
just as in etching; but instead of putting the stopping material over the whole bit
of glass and then scratching it off, as you do in copper-plate etching, it is better
for the most part to paint the stopping on where you want it, and this is
conveniently done with Brunswick black, thinned down with turpentine; if you
add a little red lead to it, it does no harm. You then treat it to a bath of fluoric
acid diluted with water and placed in a leaden pan; or, if it is only a touch you
want, you can get it off with a mop of cotton-wool on a stick, dipped in the
undiluted acid; but be careful of the fumes, for they are very acrid and
disagreeable to the eyes and nose; take care also not to get the acid on your finger-
ends or nails, especially into cuts or sore places. For protection, india-rubber
finger-stalls for finger and thumb are very good, and you can get these at any
shop where photographic materials are sold. If you do get any of the acid on to
your hands or into a cut, wash them with diluted carbonate of soda or diluted
ammonia. The acid must be kept in a gutta-percha bottle.

When the aciding is done, as far as you want it, the glass must be thoroughly
rinsed in several waters; do not leave any acid remaining, or it will continue to act
upon the glass. You must also be careful not to use this process in the
neighbourhood of any painted work, or, in short, in the neighbourhood of any
glass that is of consequence, the fumes from the acid acting very strongly and very
rapidly. This process, of course, may be used in many ways: you can, by it, acid
out a diaper pattern, red upon white, white upon red; and blue may be treated in
the same fashion; the white lights upon steel armour, for instance, may be
obtained in this way with very telling effect, getting indeed the beautiful

combination of steely blue with warm brown which we admire so in Burne-Jones cartoons; for the brown of the pigment will not show warm on the blue, but will do so directly it passes on to the white of the acided parts. This is the last process I need describe; the many little special refinements to be got by playing games with the lead lines; by thickening and thinning them; by *doubling* glass, to get depth and intensity, or to blend new tints;—these and such like are the things that any artist *who does his own work and practises his own craft* can find out, and ought to find out, and is bound to find out, for himself—they are the legitimate reward of the hand and heart labour spent, as a craftsman spends them, upon the material. Suffice it to say that in spite of the great skill which has been employed upon stained-glass, ancient and modern, and employed in enormous amount; and in spite of the great and beautiful results achieved; we may yet look upon stained-glass as an art in which there are still new provinces to explore—walking upon the old paths, guided by the old landmarks, but gathering new flowers by the way.

We must now, then, turn our attention to the mechanical processes by which the stained-glass window is finished off.

CHAPTER X

Leading-Up and Fixing—Setting out the Bench—Relation of Leading to mode of Fixing in the Stone—Process of Fixing—Leading-Up Resumed—Straightening the Lead—The "Lathykin"—The Cutting-Knife—The Nails—The Stopping-Knife—Knocking Up.

You first place your cut-line, face upward, upon the bench, and pin it down there. You next cut two "straight-edges" of wood, one to go along the base line of the section you mean to lead up, and the other along the side that lies next to you on the bench as you stand at work; for you always work *from one side*, as you will soon see. And it is important that you should get these straight-edges at a true right angle, testing them carefully with the set-square. Fig. 46 represents a bench set out for leading-up.

You must now build the glass together, as a child puts together his puzzle-map, one bit at a time, working from the base corner that is opposite your left hand.

But first of all you must place a strip of extra wide and flat lead close against each of your straight-edges, so that the core of the lead corresponds with the outside line of your work.

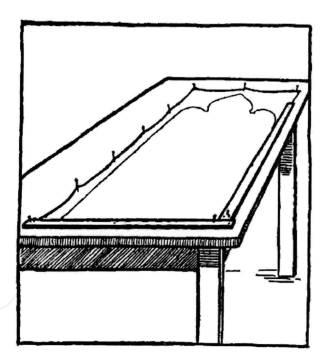

FIG. 46.

It will be right here to explain what relation the extreme outside measurement of your work should bear to the daylight sizes of the openings that it has to fill. I think we may say that, whatever the "mouldings" may be on the stone, there is always a flat piece at exact right angles to the face of the wall in which the window stands, and it is in this flat piece that the groove is cut to receive the glass (fig. 47).

FIG. 47.

Now, as the glazed light has to *fill* the daylight opening, there must obviously be a piece beyond the "daylight" size to go into the stone. By slipping the glazed light in *sideways*, and even, in large lights, by *bending* it slightly into a bow, you can just get into the stone a light an inch, or nearly so, wider than the opening; but the best way is to use an extra wide lead on the outside of your light, and bend back the outside leaf of it both front and back so that they stand at right angles to the surface of the glass (fig. 48). By this means you can reduce the size of the panel by almost 1/4 of an inch on each side; you can push the panel then, without either bending or slanting it much, up to its groove; and, putting one side as far as it will go *into* the groove, you can bend back again into their former place the two leaves of the lead on the opposite side; and when you have done that slide *them* as far as they will go into *their* groove, and do the same by the opposite pair. You will then have the panel in its groove, with about 1/4 of an inch to hold by and 1/4 of an inch of lead showing. Some people fancy an objection to this; perhaps in very small windows it might look better to have the glass "flush" with the stone; but for myself I like to see a little *showing* of that outside lead, on to which so many of the leads that cross the glass are fastened. Anyway you must bear the circumstance in mind in fixing down your straight-edges to start glazing the work; and that is why I have made this digression by mentioning now something that properly belongs to fixing.

Now before beginning to glaze you must stretch and straighten the lead; and this is done as follows (fig. 49—*Frontispiece*).

FIG. 48.

Hold the "calm" of lead in your left hand, and run the finger and thumb of your right hand down the lead so as to get the core all one way and not at all twisted: then, holding one end firmly under your right foot, take tight hold of the other end with your pliers, and pull with nearly all your force in the direction of your right shoulder. Take care not to pull in the direction of your face; for if you do, and the lead breaks, you will break some of your features also. It is very important to be careful that the lead is truly straight and not askew, otherwise, when you use it in leading, the glass will never keep flat. The next operation is to open the lead with a piece of hard wood, such as boxwood or *lignum-vitæ* (fig. 50), made to your fancy for the purpose, but something like the diagram, which glaziers call a "lathykin" (as I understand it). For cutting the lead you must have a thin knife of good steel. Some use an old dinner-knife, some a palette-knife cut down—either square across the blade or at an angle—it is a matter of taste (fig. 51).

FIG. 50.

FIG. 51.

Having laid down your leads A and B (fig. 52), put in the corner piece of glass (No. 1); two of its sides will then be covered, leaving one uncovered. Take a strip of lead and bend it round the uncovered edge, and cut it off at D, so that the end fits close and true against the *core* of lead A. And you must take notice to cut with a perfectly *vertical* cut, otherwise one side will fit close and the other will leave a gap.

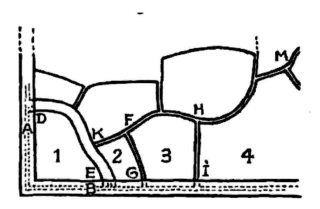

FIG. 52.

In fig. 53 A represents a good joint, B a bad one. Bend it round and cut it off similarly at E. Common sense will tell you that you must get the angle correct by marking it with a slight incision of the knife in its place before you take it on to the bench for the final cut.

Slip it in, and push it in nice and tight, and put in piece No. 2.

FIG. 53.

But now look at your cut-line. Do you see that the inner edges of pieces 2, 3, and 4 all run in a fairly smooth curve, along which a *continuous* piece of lead will bend quite easily? Leave, then, that edge, and put in, first, the leads which divide No. 2 from No. 3, and No. 3 from No. 4. Now don't forget! the long lead has to come along the inside edges of all three; so the leaf of it will overlap those three edges nearly 1/8 of an inch (supposing you are using lead of 1/4 inch dimension). You must therefore cut the two little bits we are now busy upon *1/8 of an inch short of the top edge of the glass* (fig. 54), for the inside leads only *meet* each other; it is only the *outside* lead that overlaps.

FIG. 54.

How the Loose Glass is held in its place while Leading.—This is done with nails driven into the glazing table, close up against the edge of the lead; and the best of all for the purpose are bootmakers' "lasting nails"; therefore no more need be said about the matter; "use no other" (fig. 55).

FIG. 55.

And you tap them in with two or three sharp taps; not of a hammer, for you do not want to waste time taking up a fresh tool, but with the end of your leading-knife which is called a "stopping-knife" (fig. 56), and which lead workers generally make for themselves out of an oyster-knife, by bending the blade to a convenient working angle for manipulating the lead, and graving out lines in the lower part of the handle, into which they run solder, terminating it in a solid lump at the butt-end which forms an excellent substitute for a hammer.

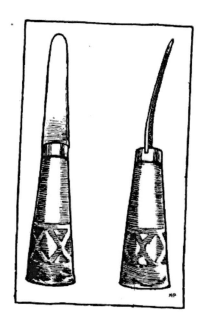

FIG. 56.

Now as soon as you have got the bits 1, 2, 3, 4 in their places, with the leads F, G and H, I between them, you can take out the nails along the line K, F, H, M, one by one as you come to them, starting from K; and put along that line one lead enclosing the whole lot, replacing the nails outside it to keep all firm as you work; and you must note that you should look out for opportunities to do this always, whenever there is a long line of the cut-line without any abrupt corners in it. You will thus save yourself the cutting (and afterwards the soldering) of unnecessary joints; for it is always good to save labour where you can without harm to the work; and in this case the work is all the better for it.

Now, when you have thus continued the leading all the way across the panel, put on the other outside lead, and so work on to a finish.

When the opposite, outside lead is put on, remove the nails and take another straight-edge and put it against the lead, and "knock it up" by hitting the straight-edge until you get it to the exact size; at the same time taking your set-square and testing the corners to see that all is at right angles.

Leave now the panel in its place, with the straight-edges still enclosing it, and solder off the joints.

CHAPTER XI

Soldering—Handling the Leaded Panel—Cementing—Recipe for Cement—The Brush—Division of Long Lights into Sections—How Joined when Fixed—Banding—Fixing—Chipping out the Old Glazing—Inserting the New and Cementing.

If the leads have got *tarnished* you may brush them over with the wire brush (fig. 57), which glaziers call a "scratch-card"; but this is a wretched business and need never be resorted to if you work with good lead and work "fresh and fresh," and finish as you go, not letting the work lie about and get stale. Take an old-fashioned tallow "dip" candle, and put a little patch of the grease over each joint, either by rubbing the candle itself on it, or by melting some of it in a saucepan and applying it with a brush. Then take your soldering-iron (fig. 58) and get it to the proper heat, which you must learn by practice, and proceed to "tin" it by rubbing it on a sheet of tin with a little solder on it, and also some resin and a little glass-dust, until the "bit" (which is of copper) has a bright tin face. Then, holding the stick of solder in the left hand, put the end of it down close to the joint you wish to solder, and put the end of the iron against it, "biting off" as it were, but really *melting* off, a little bit, which will form a liquid drop upon the joint. Spread this drop so as to seal up the joint nice and smooth and even, and the thing is done. Repeat with all the joints; then turn the panel over and do the opposite side.

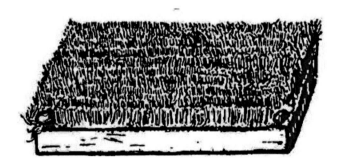

FIG. 57.

How to Handle Leaded Lights.—I said "turn the panel over." But that brings to mind a caution that you need about the handling of leaded lights. You must not—as I once saw a man do—start to hold them as a waiter does a tray. You must note that thin glass in the sheet and also leaded lights, especially before cementing, are not rigid, and cannot be handled as if they were panels of wood; you must take care, when carrying them, or when they lean against the wall, to keep them as nearly upright as they will safely stand, and the inside one leaning against a board, and not bearing its own weight. And in laying them on the bench or in lifting them off it, you must first place them so that the middle line of them corresponds with the edge of the bench, or table, and then turn them on that as an axis, quickly, so that they do not bear their own weight longer than necessary (figs. 59 and 60).

FIG. 58.

How to Cement a Leaded Light.—The next process is the cementing of the light so as to fill up the grooves of the lead and make all weather-proof. This is done with a mixture composed as follows:—Whitening, 2/3 to plaster of Paris 1/3; add a mixture of equal quantities of boiled linseed-oil and spirit of turpentine to make a paste about as thick as treacle. Add a little red lead to help to harden it, some patent dryer to cause it to dry, and lamp-black to colour.

This must be put in plenty on to the surface of the panel and well scrubbed into the joints with a hard fibre brush; an ordinary coarse "grass brush" or "bass brush," with wooden back, as sold for scrubbing brushes at the oil shops, used in all directions so as to rub the stuff into every joint.

But you must note that if you have "plated" (*i.e.* doubled) any of the glass you must, before cementing, *putty* those places. Otherwise the cement may probably run in between the two, producing blotches which you have no means of reaching in order to remove them.

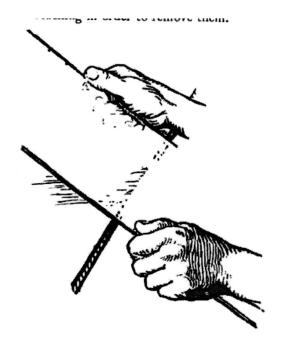

FIG. 59.

You can, if you like, clean away all the cement along the edges of the leads; but it is quite easy to be too precise and neat in the matter and make the work look hard. If you do it, a blunted awl will serve your turn.

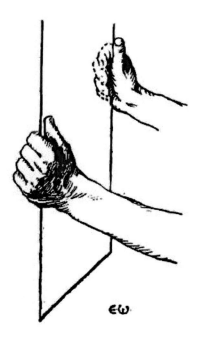

FIG. 60.

One had better mention everything, and therefore I will here say that, of course, a large light must be made in sections; and these should not exceed four feet in height, and less is better. In fixing these in their place when the window is put up (an extra wide flat lead being used at the top and bottom of each section), they are made to overlap; and if you wish the whole drainage of the window to pass into the building, of course you will put your section thus—(fig. 61 A); while if you wish the work to be weather-tight you will place it thus—(fig. 61 B). It is just as well to make every question clear if one can, and therefore I mention this. Most people like their windows weather-tight, and, of course, will make the overlapping lead the top one; but it's a free country, and I don't pretend to dictate, content if I make the situation clear to you, leaving you to deal with it according to your own fancy. All is now done except the banding.

How to Band a Leaded Light.—Banding means the putting on of the little ties of copper wire by which the window has to be held to the iron crossbars that keep it in its place. These ties are simply short lengths of copper wire, generally about four inches long, but varying, of course, with the size of the bar that you mean to use; and these are to be soldered vertically (fig. 62) on to the face of the light at any convenient places along the line where the bar will cross. In fixing the window, these wires are to be pulled tight round the bar and twisted up with pliers, and the twisted end knocked down flat and neat against the bar.

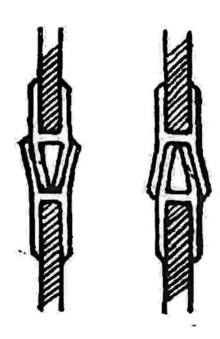

FIG. 61 A. FIG. 61 B.

And this is the very last operation in the making of a stained-glass window. It now only remains to instruct you as to what relates to the fixing of it in its place.

How to Fix a Window in its Place.—There is, almost always, a groove in the stonework to receive the glass; and, except in the case of an unfinished building, this is, of course, occupied by some form of plain glazing. You must remove this by chipping out with a small mason's chisel the cement with which it is fixed in the groove, and common sense will tell you to begin at the bottom and work upwards. This done, untwist the copper bands from the bars and put your own glass in its place, re-fixing the bars (or new ones) in the places you have determined on to suit your design and to support the glass, and fixing your glass to them in the way described, and pointing the whole with good cement. The method of inserting the new glass is described at p. 135.

But that it is good for a man to feel the satisfaction of knowing his craft thoroughly there would be no need to go into this, which, after all, is partly masons' work. But I, for my part, cannot understand the spirit of an artist who applies his art to a craft purpose and has not, at least, a strong *wish* to know all that pertains to it.

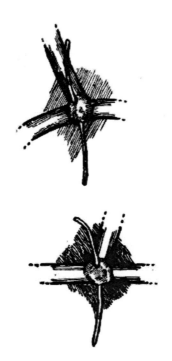

FIG. 62.

PART II

CHAPTER XII

Introductory—The Great Questions—Colour—Light—Architectural Fitness—Limitations—Thought—Imagination—Allegory.

The foregoing has been written as a handbook to use at the bench, and therefore I have tried to keep myself strictly to describing the actual processes and the ordinary practice and routine of stained-glass work.

But can we leave the subject here?

If we were speaking of even the smallest of the minor arts and crafts, we should wish to say something of why they are practised and how they should be practised, of the principles that guide them, of the spirit in which they should be undertaken, of the place they occupy in human affairs and in our life on earth. How much more then in an Art like this, which soars to the highest themes, which dares to treat, which is required to treat, of things Heavenly and Earthly, of the laws of God, and of the nature, duty, and destinies of man; and not only so, but must treat of these things in connection with, and in subservience to, the great and dominant Art of Architecture?

We must not shrink, then, from saying all that is in our mind: we must ask ourselves the great questions of all art. We must investigate the How of them, and even face the Why.

Therefore here (however hard it be to do it) something must be said of such great general principles as those of colour, of light, of architectural fitness, of limitations, of thought and imagination and allegory; for all these things belong to stained-glass work, and it is the right or wrong use of these high things that makes windows to be good or to be bad.

Let us, dear student, take the simplest things first, not because they are the easiest (though they perhaps are so), but because they will gradually, I hope, warm up our wits to the point of considering these matters, and so prepare the way for what is hardest of all.

And I think a good subject to begin with is that of Economy generally, taking into consideration both time and materials.

CHAPTER XIII

Of Economy—The Englishman's Wastefulness—Its Good Side—Its Excess—Difficulties—A Calculation—Remedies.

Those who know work in various countries must surely have arrived at the conclusion that the Englishman is the most wasteful being on the face of the globe! He only thinks of getting through the work, or whatever it may be, that he has purposed to himself, attaining the end immediately in view in the speediest manner possible without regard to anything else, lavish of himself and of the stuff he works with. The picture drawn by Robert Louis Stevenson in "Treasure Island" of John Silver and his pirates, when about to start on their expedition, throwing the remainder of their breakfast on the bivouac fire, careless whence fresh supplies might come, is "English all over." This is the character of the race. It has its good side, this grand disdain—it wins Battles, Victoria Crosses, Humane Society's medals, and other things well worth the winning; brings into port many a ship that would else be lost or abandoned, and, year in, year out, sends to sea the lifeboats on our restless line of coast. It would be something precious indeed that would be worth the loss of it; but there is a medium in all things, and when a master sees—as one now at rest once told me he often had seen—a cutter draw his diamond down a bit of the margin out of which he had just cut his piece, in order to make it small enough to throw away, without being ashamed, under the bench, he must sometimes, I should think, wish the man were employed on some warlike or adventurous trade, and that he had a Hollander or Italian in his place, who would make a whole window out of what the other casts away.

At the same time, it must be confessed that this is a very difficult matter to arrange; and it is only fair to the workman to admit that under existing conditions of work and demand, and even in many cases of the buildings in which the work is done, the way does not seem clear to have the whole of what might be wished in this matter. I will point out the difficulties against it.

First, unless some system could be invented by which the amount of glass issued to any workman could be compared easily and simply with the area of glazed work cut from it, the workman has no inducement to economise; for, no record being kept of the glass saved, he knows that he will get no credit by saving, while the extra time that he spends on economy will make him seem a slower workman, and so he would be blamed.

Then, again, it is impossible to see the colour of glass as it lies on the bench; he has little choice but to cut each piece out of the large sheet; for if he got a clutter of small bits round him till he happened to want a small bit, he would never be able to get on.

There is no use, observe, in niggling and cheese-paring. There should be a just balance made between the respective values of the man's time and the material on which it is spent; and to this end I now give some calculations to show these—

calculations rather startling, considered in the light of what one knows of the ordinary practices and methods.

The antique glasses used in stained-glass work vary in price from 1s. a foot to 5s., the weight per foot being about 32 oz.

The wage of the workmen who have to deal with this costly material varies from 8d. to 1s. per hour.

The price of the same glass thrown under the bench, and known as "cullet," is £1 per TON.

Let us now do a little simple arithmetic, which, besides its lesson to the workers, may, I think, come as a revelation even to some employers who, content with getting work done quickly, may have hardly realised the price paid for that privilege.

```
                    1 ton = 20      cwt.
                        X    4
                       80       qrs.
                        X   28
                      640
        32 oz. = 2 lb., 160
        therefore ÷ 2) 2240       lbs.
                     1120     = number of square feet in a ton.
                        The worth of this at 1s. a foot (whites) is:—
             ÷ 20) 1120       ( £56 PER TON.
                      100
                      120
                      120
       At 2s. 6d. per foot (the best of pot-metal blues, and rubies generally):—
                       56
                       56
                       28
       2-1/2 times 56 = 140      £140 PER TON.
       At 5s. a foot (gold-pink, and pale pink, venetian, and choice glasses generally):—
                       56
                        X    5
                     £280      PER TON.
```

Therefore these glasses are worth respectively—56 times, 140 times, and 280 times as much upon the bench as they are when thrown below it! And yet I ask you—employer or employed—is it not the case that, often—shall we not say "generally"?—in any given job as much goes below as remains above if the work is in fairly small pieces? Is not the accompanying diagram a fair illustration (fig. 63) of about the average relation of the shape cut to its margin of waste?

Employers estimate this waste variously. I have heard it placed as high as two-thirds; that is to say, that the glass, when leaded up, only measured one-third of the material used, or, in other words, that the workman had wasted twice as much as he used. This, I admit, was told me in my character as *customer*, and by way of explaining what I considered a high charge for work; but I suppose that no one with experience of stained-glass work would be disposed to place the amount of waste lower than one-half.

FIG. 63.

Now a good cutter will take between two and three hours to cut a square foot of average stained-glass work, fairly simple and large in scale; that is to say, supposing his pay one shilling an hour—which is about the top price—the material he deals with is about the same value as his time if he is using the cheapest glasses only. If this then is the case when the highest-priced labour is dealing only with the lowest-priced material, we may assume it as the general rule for stained-glass cutting, *on the average,* that "*labour is less costly than the material on which it is spent,*" and I would even say much less costly.

But it is not to be supposed that the little more care in avoiding waste which I am advocating would reduce his speed of work more than would be represented by twopence or threepence an hour.

But I fear that all suggestions as to mitigating this state of things are of little use. The remedy is to play into each other's hands by becoming, all of us, complete, all-round craftsmen; breaking down all the unnatural and harmful barriers that exist between "artists" and "workmen," and so fitting ourselves to take an intelligent interest in both the artistic and economic side of our work.

The possibility of this all depends on the personal relations and personal influence in any particular shop—and employers and employed must worry the question out between them. I am content with pointing out the facts.

CHAPTER XIV

Of Perfection—In Little Things—Cleanliness—Alertness—But not Hurry—Realising your Conditions-False lead lines—Shutting out Light— Bars—Their Number—Their Importance—Precedence—Observing your Limitations—A Result of Complete Training—The Special Limitations of Stained-Glass—Disguising the lead line—No full Realism—No violent Action—Self-Effacement—No Craft-Jugglery—Architectural Fitness founded on Architectural Knowledge—Seeing Work *in Situ*—Sketching in Glass—The Artistic Use of the Lead—Stepping Back—Accepting Bars and Leads—Loving Care—White Spaces to be Interesting—Bringing out the "Quality" of the Glass—Spotting and Dappling—"Builders-Glazing" *versus* Modern Restoring.

The second question of principle that I would dwell upon is that of *perfection*.

Every operation in the arts should be perfect. It has to be so in most arts, from violin-playing to circus-riding, before the artist dare make his bow to the public.

Placing on one side the question of the higher grades of art which depend upon special talent or genius—the great qualities of imagination, composition, form and colour, which belong to mastership—I would now, in this book, intended for students, dwell upon those minor things, the doing of which well or ill depends only upon good-will, patience, and industry.

Anyone can wash a brush clean; any one can keep the colour on his palette neat; can grind it all up each time it is used; can cover it over with a basin or saucer when his work is over; and yet these things are often neglected, though so easy to do. The painter will *neglect* to wash out his brush; and it will be clogged with pigment and gum, get dry, and stick to the palette, and the points of the hair will tear and break when it is removed again by the same careless hand that left it there.

Another will leave portions of his colour, caked and dry, at the edges of his palette for weeks, till all is stale; and then, when the spirit moves him, will some day work this in, full of dirt and dust, with the fresher colour. Everything, everything should be done well! From the highest forms of painting to tying up a parcel or washing out a brush;—all tools should be clean at all times, the handles as well as the hair—there is *no excuse* for the reverse; and if your tools are dirty, it is by the same defect of your character that will make you slovenly in your work. Painting does not demand the same actual *swiftness* as some other arts; nevertheless each touch that you place upon the glass, though it may be deliberate, should be deft, athletic, perfect in itself; the nerves braced, the attention keen, and the powers of soul and body as much on the alert as they would need to be in violin-playing, fencing, or dissecting.

This is not to advocate *hurry*. That is another matter altogether, for which also there is no excuse. Never hurry, or ask an assistant to hurry. Windows are delayed, even promises broken (though that can scarce be defended), there may be "ire in celestial minds"; but that is all forgotten when we are dead; and we soon shall be, but not the window.

Another thing to note, which applies generally throughout all practice, is the wisdom, of getting as near as you can to your conditions. For instance, the bits of glass in a window are separated by lead lines; pitch-black, therefore, against the light of day outside. Now, when waxed up on the plate in the shop for painting, these will be separated by thin cracks of light, and in this condition they are usually painted. Can't you do better than that? Don't you think it's worth while spending half-an-hour to paint false lead lines on the back of the plate? A ha'p'orth of lamp-black from the oil-shop, with a little water and treacle and a long-haired brush, like a coach-painter's, will do it for you (see Plate XIII.).

Another thing: when the window is in its place, each *light* will be surrounded with stone or brick, which, although not so black as the lead lines, will tell as a strong dark against the glass. See therefore that while you are painting, your glass is surrounded by dark, or at any rate not by clear, glittering light. Strips of brown paper, pinned down the sides of the light you are painting, will get the thing quite near to its future conditions.

As you have been told, the work is fixed in its place by bars of iron, and these ought by no means to be despised or ignored or disguised, as if they were a troublesome necessity: you must accept fully and willingly the conditions of your craft; you must pride yourself upon so accepting them, knowing that they are the wholesome checks upon your liberty and the proper boundaries of the field in which you have your appointed work. There should, in any light more than a foot wide, be bars at every foot throughout the length of the light; and these bars should be 1/2 inch, 3/4 inch, or 1 inch in section, according to the weight of the work. The question then arises: Should the bars be set out in their places on the paper, before you begin to draw the cartoon, or should you be perfectly free and unfettered in the drawing and then *make* the bars fit in afterwards, by moving them up and down as may be needed to avoid cutting across the faces, hands, &c.

I find more difficulty in answering this than any other *technical* question in this book. I do not think it can be answered with a hard and fast "Yes" or "No." It depends on the circumstances of the case. But I incline towards the side of making it the rule to put the bars in first, and adapt the composition to them. You may think this a surprising view for an artist to take. "Surely," you will say, "that is putting the cart before the horse, and making the more important thing give way to the less!" But my feeling is that reasonable limitations of any kind ought never to be considered as hindrances in a work of art. They are part of the problem, and it is only a spirit of dangerous license which will consider them as bonds, or will find them irksome, or wish to break them through. Stained-glass is not an independent art. It is an accessory to architecture, and any limitations imposed by structure and architectural propriety or necessity are most gravely to be considered and not lightly laid on one side. And in this connection it must be remembered that the bars cannot be made to go *anywhere* to fit a freely designed composition: they must be approximately at certain distances on account of use; and they must be arranged with regard to each other in the whole of the window on account of appearance.

You might indeed find that, in any single light, it is quite easy to arrange them at proper and serviceable distances, without cutting across the heads or hands of the figures; but it is ten chances to one that you can get them to do so, and still be level with each other, throughout a number of lights side by side.

The best plan, I think, is to set them out on the side of the cartoon-paper before you begin, but not so as to notice them; then first roughly strike out the position your most important groups or figures are to occupy, and, before you go on with the serious work of drawing, see if the bars cut awkwardly, and, if they do, whether a slight shifting of them will clear all the important parts; it often will, and then all is well; but I do not shrink from slightly altering even the position of a head or hand, rather than give a laboured look to what ought to be simple and straightforward by "coaxing" the bars up and down all over the window to fit in with the numerous heads and hands.

If, by the way, I see fit in any case to adopt the other plan, and make my composition first, placing the bars afterwards to suit it, I never allow myself to shift them from the level that is convenient and reasonable for anything *except* a head; I prefer even that they should cut across a hand, for instance, rather than that they should be placed at inconvenient intervals to avoid it.

The principle of observing your limitations is, I do not hesitate to say, the most important, and far the most important, of all principles guiding the worker in the right practising of any craft.

The next in importance to it is the right exercise of all legitimate freedom *within* those limitations. I place them in this order, because it is better to stop short, by nine-tenths, of right liberty, than to take one-tenth of wrong license. But by rights the two things should go together, and, with the requisite skill and training to use them, constitute indeed the whole of the practice of a craft.

Modern division of labour is much against both of these things, the observance of which charms us so in the ancient Gothic Art of the Middle Ages.

For, since those days, the craft has never been taught as a whole. Reader! this book cannot teach it you—no book, can; but it can make you—and it was written with the sole object of making you—*wish* to be taught it, and determine to be taught it, if you intend to practise stained-glass work at all.

Modern stained-glass work is done by numerous hands, each trained in a special skill—to design, or to paint, or to cut, or to glaze, or to fire, or to cement—but none are taught to do all; very few are taught to do more than one or two. How, then, can any either use rightful liberty or observe rightful limitations? They do not know their craft, upon which these things depend. And observe how completely also these two things depend upon each other. You may be rightly free, *because* you have rightly learnt obedience; you know your limitations, and, *therefore*, you may be trusted to think, and feel, and act for yourself.

This is what makes old glass, and indeed all old art, so full of life, so full of interest, so full of enjoyment—in places, and right places, so full even of "fun." Do you think the charming grotesques that fill up every nook and corner sometimes in the minor detail of mediæval glass or carving could ever be done by the method of a "superior person" making a drawing of them, and an inferior person laboriously translating them in *facsimile* into the material? They [P2: hyphen in facsimile is OK for 1906, the OED says that prior to 1900 fac simile (a Latin phrase) was still 2 words] are what they are because they were the spontaneous and allowed license and play of a craftsman who knew his craft, and could be trusted to use it wisely, at any rate in all minor matters.

THE LIMITATIONS OF STAINED-GLASS.

The limitations of stained-glass can only be learnt at the bench, and by years of patient practice and docile service; but it may be well to mention some of them.

You must not disguise your lead line. You must accept it willingly, as a limitation of your craft, and make it contribute to the beauty of the whole.

"But I have a light to do of the 'Good Shepherd,' and I want a landscape and sky, and how ugly lead lines look in a pale-blue sky! I get them like shapes of cloud, and still it cuts the sky up till it looks like 'random-rubble' masonry." Therefore large spaces of pale sky are "taboo," they will not do for glass, and you must modify your whole outlook, your whole composition, to suit what *will* do. If you must have sky, it must be like a Titian sky—deep blue, with well-defined masses of cloud—and you must throw to the winds resolutely all idea of attempting to imitate the softness of an English sky; and even then it must not be in a large mass: you can always break it up with branched-work of trees, or with buildings.

There should be no full realism of any kind.

No violent action must assert itself in a window.

I do not say that there must not, in any circumstances, be any violent action—the subject may demand it; but, if so, it must be so disguised by the craftsmanship of the work, or treated so decoratively, or so mixed up with the background or surroundings, that you do not see a figure in violent action starting prominently out from the window as you stand in the church. But, after all, this is a thing of artistic sense and discretion, and no rules can be formulated. The Parthenon frieze is of figures in rapid movement. Yet what repose! And in stained-glass you must aim at repose. Remember,—it is an accessory to architecture; and who is there that does not want repose in architecture? Name me a great building which does not possess it? How the architects must turn in their graves, or, if living, shake in their shoes, when they see the stained-glass man turned into their buildings, to display himself and spread himself abroad and blow his trumpet!

Efface yourself, my friend; sink yourself; illustrate the building; consider its lines and lights and shades; enrich it, complete it, make people happier to be in it.

There must be no craft-jugglery in stained-glass.

The art must set the craft simple problems; it must not set tasks that can only be accomplished by trickery or by great effort, disproportioned to the importance of the result. But, indeed, you will naturally get the habit of working according to this rule, and other reasonable rules, if you yourself work at the bench—all lies in that.

There must be nothing out of harmony with the architecture.

And, therefore, you must know something of architecture, not in order to imitate the work of the past and try to get your own mistaken for it, but to learn the love and reverence and joy of heart of the old builders, so that your spirit may harmonise with theirs.

Do not shrink from the trouble and expense of seeing the work in situ, and then, if necessary, removing it for correction and amendment.

If you have a large window, or a series of windows, to do, it is often not a very great matter to take a portion of one light at least down and try it in its place. I have done it very often, and I can assure you it is well worth while.

OF MAKING A SKETCH IN GLASS.

But there is another thing that may help you in this matter, and that is to sketch out the colour of your window in small pieces of glass—in fact, to make a scale-sketch of it in glass. A scale of one inch to a foot will do generally, but all difficult or doubtful combinations of colour should be sketched larger—full size even—before you venture to cut.

Work should be kept flat by leading.

One of the main *artistic* uses of the leadwork in a window is that, if properly used, it keeps the work flat and in one plane, and allows far more freedom in the conduct of your picture, permitting you to use a degree of realism and fulness of treatment greater than you could do without it. Work may be done, where this limitation is properly accepted and used, which would look vulgar without it; and on the other hand, the most Byzantine rigidity may be made to look vulgar if the lead line is misused. I have seen glass of this kind where the work was all on one plane, and where the artist had so far grasped proper principles as to use thick leads, but had *curved these leads in and out across the folds of the drapery as if they followed its ridges and hollows*—the thing becoming, with all its good-will to accept limitations, almost more vulgar than the discredited "Munich-glass" of a few years ago, which hated and disguised the lead lines.

You must step back to look at your work as often and as far as you can.

Respect your bars and lead lines, and let them be strong and many.

Every bit of glass in a window should look "cared for."

If there is a lot of blank space that you "don't know how to fill," be sure your design has been too narrowly and frugally conceived. I do not mean to say that there may not be spaces, and even large spaces, of plain quarry-glazing, upon which your subject with its surrounding ornament may be planted down, as a rich thing upon a plain thing. I am thinking rather of a case where you meet with some sudden lapse or gap in the subject itself or in its ornamental surroundings. This is apt specially to occur where it is one which leads rather to pictorial treatment, and where, unless you have "canopy" or "tabernacle" work, as it is called, surrounding and framing everything, you find yourself at a loss how to fill the space above or below.

Very little can be said by way of general rule about this; each case must be decided on its merits, and we cannot speak without knowing them. But two things may be said: First, that it is well to be perfectly bold (as long as you are perfectly sincere), and not be afraid, merely because they are unusual, of things that you really would like to do if the window were for yourself. There are no hard and fast rules as to what may or may not be done, and if you are a craftsman and designer also—as the whole purpose of this book is to tell you you must be—many methods will suggest themselves of making your glass look interesting. The golden rule is to handle every bit of it yourself, and then you will *be* interested in the ingenuity of its arrangement; the cutting of it into little and big bits; the lacework of the leads; thickening and thinning these also to get bold contrasts of strong and slender, of plain and intricate; catching your pearly glass like fish, in a net of larger or smaller mesh; for, bear in mind always that this question relates almost entirely to the *whiter* glasses. Colour has its own reason for being there, and carries its own interest; but the most valuable piece of advice that I can think of in regard to stained-glass *treatment* (apart from the question of subject and meaning) is to *make your white spaces interesting.*

The old painters felt this when they diapered their quarry-glazing and did such grisaille work as the "Five Sisters" window at York. Every bit of this last must have been put together and painted by a real craftsman delighting in his work. The drawing is free and beautiful; the whole work is like jewellery, the colour scheme delightfully varied and irregular. The work was loved: each bit of glass was treated on its merits as it passed through hand. Working in this way all things are lawful; you may even put a thin film of "matt" over any piece to lower it in tone and give it richness, or to bring out with emphasis some quality of its texture. Some bits will have lovely streaks and swirling lines and bands in them— "reamy," as glass-cutters call it—or groups of bubbles and spots, making the glass like agate or pebble; and a gentle hand will rub a little matt or film over these, and then finger it partly away to bring out its quality, just as a jeweller foils a stone. This is quite a different thing from smearing a window all over with dirt to make it a sham-antique; and where it is desirable to lower the tone of any white for the sake of the window, and where no special beauties of texture exist, it is better, I think, to matt it and then take out simple *patterns* from the matt: not *outlined* at all, but spotted and streaked in the matt itself, chequered and petalled and thumb-marked, just as nature spots and stripes and dapples, scatters daisies on the grass and snowflakes in the air, and powders over with chessboard chequers and lacings and "oes and eyes of light," the wings of butterflies and birds.

So man has always loved to work when he has been let to choose, and when nature has had her way. Such is the delightful art of the basket and grass-cloth weaver of the Southern seas; of the ancient Cyprian potter, the Scandinavian and the Celt. It never dies; and in some quiet, merciful time of academical neglect it crops up again. Such is the, often delightful, "builders-glazing" of the "carpenters-Gothic" period, or earlier, when the south transept window at Canterbury, and the east and west windows at Cirencester, and many such like, were rearranged with old materials and new by rule of thumb and just as the glazier "thought he would." Heaven send us nothing worse done through too much learning! I daresay he shouldn't have done it; but as it came to him to do, as, probably, he was ordered to do it, we may be glad he did it just so. In the Canterbury window, for instance, no doubt much of the old glass never belonged to that particular window; it may have been, sinfully, brought there from windows where it did belong. At Cirencester there are numbers of bits of canopy and so forth, delightful fifteenth-century work, exquisitely beautiful, put in as best they could be; no doubt from some mutilated window where the figures had been destroyed—for, if my memory serves me, most of them have no figures beneath—and surrounded by little chequered work, and stripes and banding of the glaziers' own fancy. A modern restorer would have delighted to supply sham-antique saints for them, imitating fifteenth-century work (and deceiving nobody), and to complete the mutilated canopies by careful matching, making the window entirely correct and uninteresting and lifeless and accomplished and forbidding. The very blue-bottles would be afraid to buzz against it; whereas here, in the old church, with the flavour of sincerity and simplicity around them, at one with the old carving and the spirit of the old time, they glitter with fresh feeling, and hang there, new and old together, breaking sunlight; irresponsible, absurd, and delightful.

CHAPTER XV

A Few Little Dodges—A Clumsy Tool—A Substitute—A Glass Rack—
An Inconvenient Easel—A Convenient Easel—A Waxing-up Tool—An
Easel with Movable Plates—Making the most of a Room—Handling
Cartoons—Cleanliness—Dust—The   Selvage   Edge—Drying   a
"Badger"—A Comment.

Here, now, follow some little practical hints upon work in general; mere
receipts; description of time-saving methods and apparatus which I have
separated from the former part of the book; partly because they are mostly
exceptions to the ordinary practice, and partly because they are of general
application, the common-sense of procedure, and will, I hope, after you have
learnt from the former parts of the book the individual processes and operations,
help you to marshal these, in order and proportion, so as to use them to the
greatest advantage and with the best results. And truly our stained-glass methods
are most wasteful and bungling. The ancient Egyptians, they say, made glass, and
I am sure some of our present tools and apparatus date from the time of the
Pyramids.

A CLUMSY KILN-FEEDER.

What shall we say, for instance, of this instrument (fig. 64), used for loading
some forms of kiln?

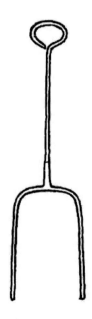

FIG. 64.

The workman takes the ring-handle in his right hand, rests the shaft in the crook of his left elbow, puts the fork under an iron plate loaded with glass and weighing about forty pounds, and then, with tug and strain, lifts it, ready to slip off and smash at any moment, and, grunting, transfers it to the kiln. A little mechanical appliance would save nine-tenths of the labour, a stage on wheels raised or lowered at will (a thing which surely should not be hard to invent) would bring it from the bench to the kiln, and *then*, if needs be, and no better method could be found, the fork might be used to put it in.

Meanwhile, as a temporary step in the right direction, I illustrate a little apparatus invented by Mr. Heaton, which, with the tray made of some lighter substance than iron, of which he has the secret, decreases the labour by certainly one-third, and I think a half (fig. 65).

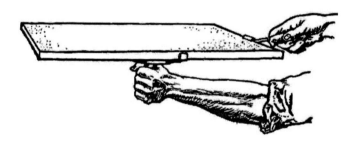

FIG. 65.

It is indeed only a sort of half-way house to the right thing, but, tested one against the other with equal batches of plates, its use is certainly less laborious than that of the fork. And that is a great gain; for the consequence of these rough ways is that the kiln-man, whom we want to be a quiet, observant man, with plenty of leisure and with all his strength and attention free to watch the progress of a process or experiment, like a chemist in his laboratory, has often two-thirds of it distracted by the stress of needless work which is only fit for a navvy, and the only tendency of which can be towards turning him into one.

A GLASS-RACK FOR WASTE PIECES.

Then the cutter, who throws away half the stuff under his bench! How easy it would be, if things were thought of from the beginning and the place built for the work, to have such width of bench and space of window that, along the latter, easily and comfortably within reach, should run stages, tier above tier, of strong sheet or thin plate glass, sloping at such an angle that the cuttings might lie along them against the light, with a fillet to stop them from falling off. Then it would be a pleasure, as all handy things are, for the workman to put his bits of glass there, and when he wanted a piece of similar colour, to raise his head and choose one, instead of wastefully cutting a fresh piece out of the unbroken sheet, or wasting his time rummaging amongst the bits on the bench. A stage on the same principle for *choosing* glass is illustrated in fig. 67.

But it is in easels that improvement seems most wanted and would be most easy, and here I really must tell you a story.

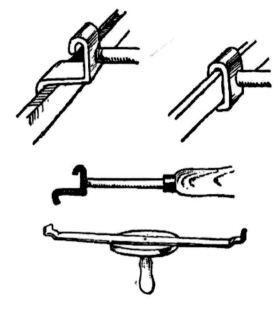

FIG. 66.

AN INCONVENIENT EASEL.

Having once some very large lights to paint, against time, the friends in whose shop I was to work (wishing to give me every advantage and to *save time*), had had special easels made to take in the main part of each light at once. But an "Easel," in stained-glass work, meaning always the single slab of plate-glass in a wooden frame, these were of that type. I forget their exact size and could hazard no guess at their weight, but it took four men to get one from the ground on to the bench. Why, I wanted it done a dozen times an hour! and should have wished to be able to do it at any moment. Instead of that it was, "Now then, Bill; ease her over!" "Steady!" "Now lift!" "All together, boys!" and so forth. I wonder there wasn't a strike! But did no one, then, ever see in a club or hotel a plate-glass window about as big as a billiard-table, and a slim waiter come up to it, and, with a polite "Would you like the window open, sir?" quietly lift it with one hand?

FIG. 67.

A CONVENIENT EASEL.

Fig. 68 is a diagram of the kind of easel I would suggest. It can either stand on the bench or on the floor, and with the touch of a hand can be lifted, weighing often well over a hundredweight, to any height the painter pleases, till it touches the roof, enabling him to see at any moment the whole of his work at a distance and against the sky, which one would rather call an absolute necessity than a mere convenience or advantage.

Some of these things were thought out roughly by myself, and have been added to and improved from time to time by my painters and apprentices, a matter which I shall say a word on by-and-by, when we consider the relations which should exist between these and the master.

AN IMPROVED TOOL FOR WAXING-UP.

Meanwhile here is another little tool (fig. 69), the invention of one of my youngest "hands" (and heads), and really a praiseworthy invention, though indeed a simple and self-evident matter enough. The usual tool for waxing-up is (1) a strip of glass, (2) a penknife, (3) a stick of wood. The thing most to be wished for in whatever is used being, of course, that it *should retain the heat*. This youth argued: "If they use copper for soldering-bits because it retains heat so well, why not use copper for the waxing-up tool? besides, it can be made into a pen which will hold more wax."

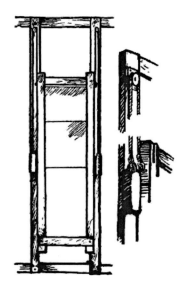

FIG. 68.

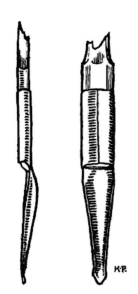

FIG. 69.

So said, so done; nothing indeed to make a fuss about, but part of a very wholesome spirit of wishing to work with handy tools economically, instead of blundering and wasting.

AN EASEL WITH MOVABLE PLATES.

But to return for a moment to the easel. I find it very convenient not to have it made all of one plate of glass, but to divide it so that about four plates make the whole easel of five feet high. These plates slip in grooves, and can be let in either at the top or bottom, the latter being then stopped by a batten and thumbscrews. By this means a light of any length can be painted in sections without a break. For supposing you work from below upwards, and have done the first five feet of the window, take out all the glass except the top plate, *shift this down to the bottom*, and place three empty plates above it, and you can join the upper work to the lower by the sample of the latter left in its place to start you.

HOW TO MAKE THE MOST OF A ROOM.

The great point is to be able to get away as far as you can from your work. And I advise you, if your room is small, to have a fair-sized mirror (a cheval-glass) and place it at the far end of your room opposite the easel where you are painting, and then, standing close by the side of your easel, look at your work in the mirror. This will double the distance at which you see it, and at the same time present it to you reversed; which is no disadvantage, for you then see everything under a fresh aspect and so with a fresh eye. Of course, by the use of two mirrors, if they be large enough, you can put your work away to any distance. You must have seen this in a restaurant where there were mirrors, and where you have had presented to you an endless procession of your own head, first front then back, going away into the far distance.

HOW TO HANDLE CARTOONS.

Well, it's really like insulting your intelligence! And if I hadn't seen fellows down on their hands and knees rolling and unrolling cartoons along the dirty floor, and sprawling all over the studio so that everybody had to get out of the way into corners, I wouldn't spend paper and ink to tell you that by standing the roll *upright* and spinning it gently round with your hands, freeing first one edge and then another, you can easily and quietly unroll and sort out a bundle of a dozen cartoons, each twenty feet long, on the space of a small hearth-rug; but so it is (fig. 70), and in just the same way you can roll them up again.

NEATNESS AND CLEANLINESS.

You should have drawers in the tables, and put the palettes away in these with the colour neatly covered over with a basin when you leave work. Dust is a great enemy in a stained-glass shop, and it must be kept at arm's length.

YOU MUST TEAR OFF THE SELVAGE EDGE OF YOUR TRACING CLOTH,

otherwise the tracing cloth being all cockled at the edge, which, however, is not very noticeable, will not lie flat, and you will be puzzled to know why it is that you cannot get your cut-line straight; tear off the edge, and it lies perfectly flat, without a wrinkle.

HOW TO DRY A BIG BRUSH OR BADGER AFTER IT IS WASHED.

I expect you'd try to dry it in front of the fire, and there'd be a pretty eight-shilling frizzle! But the way is this: First sweep the wet brush downwards with all your force, just as you shake the worst of the wet off a dripping umbrella, then take the handle of the brush *between the palms of your hands*, with the hair pointing downwards, and rub your hands smartly together, with the handle between them, just as an Italian waiter whisks up the chocolate. This sends the hair all out like a Catherine-wheel, and dries the brush with quite astonishing rapidity. Come now! you'd never have thought of that?

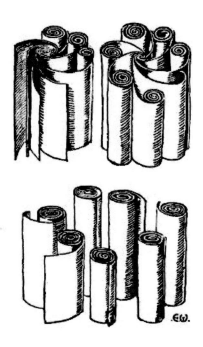

FIG. 70.

And why have I reserved these hints till now? surely these are things of the work-bench, practical matters, and would have come more conveniently in their own place? Why have I—do you ask—after arousing your attention to the "great principles of art," gone back again all at once to these little matters?

Dear reader, I have done so deliberately to emphasise the *First* of principles, that the right learning of any craft is the learning it under a master, and that all else is makeshift; to drive home the lesson insisted on in the former volumes of this series of handbooks, and gathered into the sentence quoted as a motto on the fly-leaf of one of them, that "An art can only be learned in the workshop of those who are winning their bread by it."

These little things we have just been speaking of occurred to me after the practical part was all written; and I determined, since it happened so, to put them by themselves, to point this very lesson. They are just typical instances of hundreds of little matters which belong to the bench and the workshop, and which cannot all be told in any book; and even if told can never be so fully grasped as they would be if shown by master to pupil. Years—centuries of practice have made them the commonplaces of the shops; things told in a word and learnt in an instant, yet which one might go on for a whole lifetime without thinking of, and for lack of which our lifetime's work would suffer.

Man's work upon earth is all like that. The things are there under his very nose, but he never discovers them till some accident shows them; how many centuries of sailing, think you, passed by before men knew that the tides went with the moon?

Why then write a book at all, since it is not the best way?

Speaking for myself only, the reasons appear to be: First, because none of these crafts is at present taught in its fulness in any ordinary shop, and I would wish to give you at least a longing to learn yours in that fulness; and, second, because it seems also very advisable to interest the general reader in this question of the complete teaching of the crafts to apprentices. To insist on the value and necessity of the daily and hourly lessons that come from the constant presence, handling, and use of all the tools and materials, all the apparatus and all the conditions of the craft, and from the interchange of ideas amongst those who are working, side by side, making fresh discoveries day by day as to what materials will do under the changes that occur in conditions that are ever changing.

However, one must not linger further over these little matters, and it now becomes my task to return to the great leading principles and try to deal with them, and the first cardinal principle of stained-glass work surely is that of COLOUR.

CHAPTER XVI

OF COLOUR

But how hopeless to deal with it by way of words in a book where actual colour cannot be shown!

Nevertheless, let us try.

...One thinks of morning and evening;...of clouds passing over the sun; of the dappled glow and glitter, and of faint flushes cast from the windows on the cathedral pavement; of pearly white, like the lining of a shell; of purple bloom and azure haze, and grass-green and golden spots, like the budding of the spring; of all the gaiety, the sparkle, and the charm.

And then, as if the evening were drawing on, comes over the memory the picture of those graver harmonies, in the full glow of red and blue, which go with the deep notes of the great organ, playing requiem or evening hymn.

Of what use is it to speak of these things? The words fall upon the ear, but the eye is not filled.

All stained-glass gathers itself up into this one subject; the glory of the heavens is in it and the fulness of the earth, and we know that the showing forth of it cannot be in words.

Is it any use, for instance, to speak of these primroses along the railway bank, and those silver buds of the alder in the hollow of the copse?

One thinks of a hint here and a hint there; the very sentences come in fragments. Yet one thing we may say securely: that the practice of stained-glass is a very good way to *learn* colour, or as much of it as can come by learning.

For, consider:—

A painter has his colour-box and palette;

And if he has a good master he may learn by degrees how to mix his colour into harmonies;

Doing a little first, cautiously;

Trying the problem in one or two simple tints; learning the combinations of these in their various degrees of lighter or darker:

Exhausting, as much as he can, the possibilities of one or two pigments, and then adding another and another;

But always with a very limited number of actual separate ones to draw upon;

All the infinity of the whole world of colour being in his own hands, and the difficulty of dealing with it laid as a burden upon his own shoulders, as he combines, modifies, mixes, and dilutes them.

He perhaps has eight or ten spots of pure colour, ranged round his palette; and all the rest depends upon himself.

This gives him, indeed, one side of the practice of his art; and if he walks warily, yet daringly, step by step, learning day by day something more of the powers that lie in each single kind of paint, and as he learns it applying his knowledge, bravely and industriously, to add strength to strength, brightness to brightness, richness to richness, depth to depth, in ever clearer, fuller, and more gorgeous harmony, he may indeed become a great painter.

But a more timid or indolent man gets tired or afraid of putting the clear, sharp tints side by side to make new combinations of pure and vivid colour.

And even a man industrious, alert, and determined may lose his way and get confused amongst the infinity of choice, through being badly taught, and especially through being allowed at first too great a range, too wide a choice, too lavish riches.

A man so trained, so situated, so tempted, stands in danger of being contented to repeat old receipts and formulas over and over, as soon as he has acquired the knowledge of a few.

Or, bewildered with the lavishness of his means and confused in his choice, tends to fall into indecision, and to smear and dilute and weaken.

I cannot help thinking that it is to this want of a system of gradual teaching of the elementary stages of colour in painting that we owe, on the one side, the fashion of calling irresolute and undecided tints "art" colours; and, on the other hand, the garishness of our modern exhibitions compared with galleries of old paintings. For Titian's burning scarlet and crimson and palpitating blue; and Veronese's gold and green and white and rose are certainly not "art colours"; and I think we must feel the justice and truth of Ruskin's words spoken regarding a picture of Linnell's:—

"And what a relief it is for any wholesome human sight, after sickening itself among the blank horror of dirt, ditchwater, and malaria, which the imitators of the French schools have begrimed our various Exhibition walls with, to find once more a bit of blue in the sky and a glow of brown in the coppice, and to see that Hoppers in Kent can enjoy their scarlet and purple—like Empresses and Emperors." (Ruskin, "Royal Academy Notes," 1875.)

From this irresolution and indecision and the dull-colour school begotten of it on the one hand, and from garishness on the other, stained-glass is a great means of salvation; for in practising this art the absolute judgment must, day by day, be exercised between this and that colour, there present before it; and the will is braced by the necessity of constant choice and decision. In short, by many of the modern, academical methods of teaching painting, and especially by the unfortunate arrangement, where it exists, of a pupil passing under a succession of different masters, I fear the colour-sense is perplexed and blunted; while by stained-glass, taught, as all art should be, from master to apprentice, while both make their bread by it, the colour-sense would be gradually and steadily cultivated and would have time to grow.

This at least seems certain: that all painters who have also done stained-glass, or indeed any other decorative work in colour, get stronger and braver in painting from its practice. So worked Titian, Giorgione, Veronese; and so in our days worked Burne-Jones, Rossetti, Madox-Brown, Morris; and if I were to advise and prate about what is, perhaps, not my proper business, I would say, even to the student of oil-painting, "Begin with burnt-umber, trying it in every degree with white; transparent over opaque and opaque over transparent; trying how near you can get to purple and orange by contrast (and you will get nearer than you think); then add sienna at one end and black at the other to enlarge the range;—and then get a set of glass samples".

I have said that stained-glass is "a great means of salvation," from irresolution and indecision on the one hand and from garishness on the other; but it is only a means—the fact of salvation lies always in one's own hands—for we must, I fear, admit that "garishness" and "irresolution" are not unknown in stained-glass itself, in spite of the resources and safeguardings we have attributed to the material. Speaking, therefore, now to stained-glass painters themselves, we might say that these faults in their own art, as too often practised in our days, arise, strange as it may seem, from ignorance of their own material, that very material the *knowledge* of which we have just been recommending as a safeguard against these very faults to the students of another art.

And this brings us back to our subject.

For the foregoing discussion of painters' methods has all been written to draw a comparison and emphasise a contrast.

A contrast from which you, student of stained-glass, I hope may learn much.

For as we have tried to describe the methods of the painter in oil or water colours, and so point out his advantages and disadvantages, so we would now draw a picture of the glass-painter at work; if he works as he should do.

For the painter of pictures (we said) has his colour-box of a few pigments, from which all his harmonies must come by mixing them and diluting them in various proportions, dealing with infinity out of a very limited range of materials, and required to supply all the rest by his own skill and memory.

Coming each day to his work with his palette clean and his colours in their tubes;

Beginning, as it were, all over again each time; and perhaps with his heart cold and his memory dull.

But the glass-painter has his specimens of glass round him; some hundreds, perhaps, of all possible tints.

He has, with these, to compose a subject in colour;

There is no getting out of it or shirking it;

He places the bits side by side, with no possibility (which the palette gives) of slurring or diluting or dulling them; he must choose from the clear hard tints;

And he has the whole problem before him;

He removes one and substitutes another;

"This looks better;" "That is a pleasant harmony;" "Ah! but this makes it sing!"

He gets them into groups, and combines them into harmonies, tint with tint, group with group:

If he is wise he has them always by him;

Always ready to arrange in a movable frame against the window;

He cuts little bits of each; he waxes them, or gums them, into groups on sheets of glass;

He tries all his effects in the glass itself; he sketches in glass.

If he is wise he does this side by side with his water-colour sketch, making each help the other, and thinking in glass; even perhaps making his water-colour sketch afterwards from the glass.

Is it not reasonable?

Is it not far more easy, less dangerous?

He has not to rake in his cold and meagre memory to fish out some poor handful of all the possible harmonies;

To repeat himself over and over again.

He has all the colours burning round him; singing to him to use them; sounding all their chords.

Is it not the way? Is it not common sense?

Tints! pure tints! What great things they are.

I remember an old joke of the pleasant Du Maurier, a drawing representing two fashionable ladies discussing the afternoon's occupation. One says: "It's quite too dull to see colours at Madame St. Aldegonde's; suppose we go to the Old Masters' Exhibition!"

Rather too bad! but the ladies were not so altogether frivolous as might at first appear. I am afraid *Punch* meant that they were triflers who looked upon colour in dress as important, and colour in pictures as a thing which would do for a dull day. But they were not quite so far astray as this! There are other things in pictures besides colour which can be seen with indifferent light. But to match clear tint against clear tint, and put together harmonies, there is no getting away from the problem! It is all sheer, hard exercise; you want all your light for it; there is no slurring or diluting, no "glazing" or "scumbling," and it should form a part of the teaching, and yet it never does so, in our academies and schools of art. A curious matter this is, that a painter's training leaves this great resource of knowledge neglected, leaves the whole thing to memory. Out of all the infinite possible harmonies only getting what rise in the mind at the moment from the unseen. While ladies who want to dress beautifully look at the things themselves, and compare one with another. And how nicely they dress. If only painters painted half as well. If the pictures in our galleries only looked half as harmonious as the crowd of spectators below them! I would have it part of every painter's training to practise some craft, or at least that branch of some craft, which compels the choosing and arranging, in due proportions for harmony, of clear, sharp glowing colours in some definite material, from a full and lavish range of existing samples. It is true that here and there a painter will arise who has by nature that kind of instinct or memory, or whatever it is, that seems to feel harmonies beforehand, note by note, and add them to one another with infallible accuracy; but very few possess this, and for those who lack I am urging this training. For it is a case of

"the little more and how much it is,
And the little less and what worlds away."

Millais hung a daring crimson sash over the creamy-white bed-quilt, in the glow of the subdued night-lamp, in his picture of "Asleep," and we all thought what a fine thing it was. But we have not thought it so fine for the whole art world to burst into the subsequent imitative paroxysm of crashing discords in chalk, lip-salve, and skim-milk, which has lasted almost to this day.

At any rate, I throw out this hint for pupils and students, that if they will get a set of glass samples and try combinations of colour in them, they will have a bracing and guiding influence, the strength of which they little dream of, regarding one of the hardest problems of their art.

This for the student of painting in general: but for the glass-painter it is absolutely essential—the central point, the breath-of-life of his art.

To live in it daily and all day.

To be ever dealing with it thus.

To handle with the hands constantly.

To try this piece, and that piece, the little more and the little less.

This is the be-all and end-all, the beginning and the end of the whole matter, and here therefore follow a few hints with regard to it.

And there is one rule of such dominating importance that all other hints group themselves round it; and yet, strangely enough, I cannot remember seeing it anywhere written down.

Take three tints of glass—a purple, let us say, a crimson, and a green.

Let it be supposed that, for some reason, you desire that this should form a scheme of colour for a window, or part of a window, with, of course, in addition, pure white, and probably some tints more neutral, greenish-whites and olives or greys, for background.

You choose your purple (and, by-the-bye, almost the only way to get a satisfactory one, except by a happy accident now and then, is to double gold-pink with blue; this is the only way to get a purple that will vibrate, palpitating against the eye like the petal of a pansy in the sun). Well, you get your purple, and you get your green—not a sage-green, or an "art-green," but a cold, sharp green, like a leaf of parsley, an aquamarine, the tree in the "Eve" window at Fairford, grass in an orchard about sunset, or a railway-signal lamp at night.

Your crimson like a peony, your white like white silk; and now you are started.

You put slabs of these—equal-sized samples, we will suppose—side by side, and see "if they will do."

And they don't "do" at all.

Take away the red.

The green and the purple do well enough, and the white.

But you *want* the red, you say.

Well, *put back a tenth part of it.*

And how now?

Add a still smaller bit of pale pink.

And how now?

Do you see what it all means? It means the rule we spoke of, and which we may as well, therefore, now announce:

"HARMONY IN COLOUR DEPENDS NOT ONLY UPON THE ARRANGING OF RIGHT COLOURS TOGETHER, BUT THE ARRANGING OF THE RIGHT QUANTITIES AND THE RIGHT DEGREES OF THEM TOGETHER."

To which may be added another, *à propos* of our bit of "pale pink."

THE HARSHEST CONTRASTS, EVEN DISCORDS, MAY OFTEN BE BROUGHT INTO HARMONY BY ADDED NOTES.

I believe that these are the two, and I would even almost say the only two, great leading principles of the science of colour, as used in the service of Art; and we might learn them, in all their fulness, in a country walk, if we were simple enough to like things because we like them, and let the kind nurse, Nature, take us by the hand. This very problem, to wit: Did you never see a purple anemone? against its green leaves? with a white centre? and with a thin ring of crimson shaded off into pink? And did you never wonder at its beauty, and wonder how so simple a thing could strike you almost breathless with pure physical delight and pleasure? No doubt you did; but you probably may not have asked yourself whether you would have been equally pleased if the purple, green, and red had all been equal in quantity, and the pale pink omitted.

I remember especially in one particular window where this colour scheme was adopted—an "Anemone-coloured" window—the modification of the one splash of red by the introduction of a lighter pink which suggested itself in the course of work as it went along, and was the pet fancy of an assistant—readily accepted.

The window in question is small and in nowise remarkable, but it was in the course of a ride taken to see it in its place, on one of those glorious mornings when Spring puts on all the pageantry of Summer, that the thoughts with which we are now dealing, and especially the thoughts of the infinite suggestion which Nature gives in untouched country and of the need we have to drink often at that fountain, were borne in upon the writer with more than usual force.

To take in fully and often the glowing life and strength and renewal direct from Nature is part of every man's proper manhood, still more then of every artist's artistry and student's studentship.

And truly 'tis no great hardship to go out to meet the salutary discipline when the country is beautiful in mid-April, and the road good and the sun pleasant. The Spring air sets the blood racing as you ride, and when you stop and stand for a moment to enjoy these things, ankle-deep in roadside grass, you can seem to hear the healthy pulses beating and see the wavy line of hills beating with them, as you look at the sun-warmed world.

It is good sometimes to think where we are in the scheme of things, to realise that we are under the bell-glass of this balmy air, which shuts us in, safe from the pitch-dark spaces of infinite cold, through which the world is sweeping at eighteen miles a second; while we, with all our little problems to solve and work to do, are riding warm by this fireside, and the orange-tip butterflies with that curious pertinacity of flight which is speed without haste are keeping up their incessant, rippling patrol, to and fro along the length of every sunny lane, above the ditch-side border of white-blossomed keck!

What has all this to do with stained-glass?

Everything, my boy! Be a human! For you have got to choose your place in things, and to choose on which side you will work.

A choice which, in these days, more than ever perhaps before, is one between such things as these and the money-getting which cares so little for them. I have tried to show you one side by speaking of a little part of what may be seen and felt on a spring morning, along a ridge of untouched hills in "pleasant Hertfordshire:" if you want to see the other side of things ride across to Buntingford, and take the train back up the Lea Valley. Look at Stratford (and smell it) and imagine it spreading, as no doubt it will, where its outposts of oil-mill and factory have already led the way, and think of the valley full up with slums, from Lea Bridge to Ponders End! For the present writer can remember—and that not half a lifetime back—Edmonton and Tottenham, Brondesbury and Upton Park, sweet country villages where quiet people lived and farmed and gardened amidst the orchards, fields, and hawthorn lanes.

Here now live, in mile after mile of jerry-building, the "hands" who, never taught any craft or work worthy of a man, spend their lives in some little single operation that, as it happens, no machine has yet been invented to perform; month after month, year after year, painting, let us say, endless repeats of one pattern to use as they are required for the borders of pious windows in the churches of this land.

This is the "other side of things," much commended by what is looked on as "robust common sense"; and with this you have—nothing to do. Your place is elsewhere, and if it needs be that it seems an isolated one, you must bear it and accept it. Nature and your craft will solve all; live in them, bathe in them to the lips; and let nothing tempt you away from them to measure things by the standard of the mart.

Let us go back to our sunny hillside. "It is good for us to be here," for this also is Holy Ground; and you must indeed be much amongst such things if you would do stained-glass, for you will never learn all the joy of it in a dusty shop.

"So hard to get out of London?"

But get a bicycle then;—only sit upright on it and go slow—and get away from these bricks and mortar, to where we can see things like these! those dandelions and daisies against the deep, green grass; the blazing candles of the sycamore buds against the purple haze of the oak copse; and those willows like puffs of grey smoke where the stream winds. Did you ever? No, you never! Well—do it then!

But indeed, having stated our *principles* of colour, the practice of those principles and the influence of nature and of nature's hints upon that practice are infinite, both in number and variety. The flowers of the field and garden; butterflies, birds, and shells; the pebbles of the shore; above all, the dry seaweeds, lying there, with the evening sun slanting through them. These last are exceedingly like both in colour and texture, or rather in colour and the amount of translucency, to fine old stained-glass; so also are dead leaves. But, in short, the thing is endless. The "wine when it is red" (or amber, as the case may be), even the whisky and water, and whisky *without* water, side by side, make just those straw and ripe-corn coloured golden-yellows that are so hard to attain in stained-glass (impossible indeed by means of yellow-stain), and yet so much to be desired and sought after.

Will you have more hints still? Well, there are many tropical butterflies, chiefly among the *Pierinf*, with broad spaces of yellow dashed with one small spot or flush of vivid orange or red. Now you know how terrible yellow and red may be made to look in a window; for you have seen "ruby" robes in conjunction with "yellow-stain," or the still more horrible combination where ruby has been acided off from a yellow base. But it is a question of the actual quality of the two tints and also of their quantity. What I have spoken of looks horrible because the yellow is of a brassy tone, as stain so often is, especially on green-white glasses, and the red inclining to puce—jam-colour. It is no use talking, therefore, of "red and yellow"—we must say *what* red and *what* yellow, and how much of each. A magenta-coloured dahlia and a lemon put together would set, I should think, any teeth on edge; yet ripe corn goes well with poppies, but not too many poppies— while if one wing of our butterfly were of its present yellow and the other wing of the same scarlet as the spot, it would be an ugly object instead of one of the delights of God. It is interesting, it is fascinating to take the hint from such things—to splash the golden wings of your Resurrection Angel as he rolls away the stone with scarlet beads of sunrise, not seen but *felt* from where you stand on the pavement below. I want the reader to fully grasp this question of *quantity*, so I will instance the flower of the mullein which contains almost the very tints of the "lemon," and the "dahlia" I quoted, and yet is beautiful by virtue of its *quantities*: which may be said to be of a "lemon" yellow and yet can bear (ay! can it *not?*) the little crimson stamens in the heart of it and its sage-green leaves around.

And there is even something besides "tint" and "quantity." The way you *distribute* your colour matters very much. Some in washes, some in splashes, some in spots, some in stripes. What will "not do" in one way will often be just right in the other: yes, and the very way you treat your glass when all is chosen and placed together—matt in one place, film in another, chequering, cross-hatching, clothing the raw glass with texture and bringing out its nature and its life.

Do not be afraid; for the things that yet remain to do are numberless. Do you like the look of deep vivid vermilion-red, upon dark cold green? Look at the hip-loaded rose-briar burning in the last rays of a red October sunset! You get physical pleasure from the sight; the eye seems to vibrate to the harmony as the ear enjoys a chord struck upon the strings. Therefore do not fear. But mind, it must be in nature's actual colour, not merely "green" and "red": for I once saw the head of a celebrated tragic actress painted by a Dutch artist who, to make it as deathly as he could, had placed the ashen face upon a background of emerald-green with spots of actual red sealing-wax. The eye was so affected that the colours swung to and fro, producing in a short time a nausea like sea-sickness. That is not pleasure.

The training of the colour-sense, like all else, should be gradual; springing as it were from small seed. Be reticent, try small things first. You are not likely to be asked to do a great window all at once, even if you have the misfortune to be an independent artist approaching this new art without a gradual training under the service of others. Try some simple scheme from the things of Nature. Hyacinths look well with their leaves: therefore *that* green and *that* blue, with the white of April clouds and the black of the tree-stems in the wood are colours that can be used together.

You must be prepared to find almost a sort of penalty in this habit of looking at everything with the eye of a stained-glass artist. One seems after a time to see natural objects with numbers attached to them corresponding with the numbers of one's glasses in the racks: butterflies flying about labelled "No. 50, deep," or "75*a*, pale," or a bit of "123, special streaky" in the sunset. But if one does not obtrude this so as to bore one's friends, the little personal discomfort, if it exists, is a very small price to pay for the delight of living in this glorious fairyland of colour.

Do not think it beneath your dignity or as if you were shirking some vital artistic obligation, to take hints from these natural objects, or from ancient or modern glass, in a perfectly frank and simple manner; nay, even to match your whole colour scheme, tint for tint, by them if it seems well to you. You may get help anywhere and from anything, and as much as you like; it will only be so much more chance for you; so much richer a store to choose from, so much stronger resource to guide to good end; for after all, with all the helps you can get, much lies in the doing. Do what you like then—as a child: but be sure you *do* like it: and if the window wants a bit of any particular tint, put it there, meaning or no meaning. If there is no robe or other feature to excuse and account for it in the spot which seems to crave for it,—put the colour in, anywhere and anyhow—in the background if need be—a sudden orange or ruby "quarry" or bit of a quarry, as if the thing were done in purest waywardness. "You would like a bit there if there were an excuse for it?" Then there *is* an excuse—the best of all—that the eye demands it. Do it fearlessly.

But to work in this way (it hardly need be said) you must watch and work at your glass yourself; for these hints come late on in the work, when colour, light and shade, and design are all fusing together into a harmony. You can no more forecast these final accidents, which are the flower and crown and finish of the whole, than you could forecast the lost "Chord";—

"Which came from the soul of the organ,
And entered into mine."

It "comes from the soul" of the window.

We all know the feeling—the climaxes, exceptions, surprises, suspensions, in which harmony delights; the change from the last bar of the overture to the first of the opening recitative in the "Messiah," the chord upon which the victor is crowned in "The Meistersingers," the 59th and 60th bars in Handel's "Every Valley." (I hope some of us are "old-fashioned" enough to be unashamed of still believing in Handel!)

Or if it may be said that these are hardly examples of the kind of accidental things I have spoken of, being rather, indeed, the deliberately arranged climax to which the whole construction has been leading, I would instance the 12th (complete) bar in the overture to "Tannhäuser," the 20th and 22nd bar in Chopin's Funeral March, the change from the minor to major in Schubert's Romance from "Rosamunde," and the 24th bar in his Serenade (*Ständchen*), the 13th and following bars of the Crescendo in the Largo Appassionato of Beethoven's Op. 2. Or if you wish to have an example where *all* is exception, like one of the south nave windows in York Minster, the opening of the "Sonata Appassionata," Op. 57.

Now how can you forecast such things as these!

Let me draw another instance from actual practice. I was once painting a figure of a bishop in what I meant to be a dark green robe, the kind of black, and yet vivid, green of the summer leafage of the oak; for it was St. Boniface who cut down the heathen oak of Frisia. But the orphreys of his cope were to be embroidered in gold upon this green, and therefore the pattern had first to be added out in white upon a blue-flashed glass, which yellow stain over all would afterwards turn into green and gold. And when all was prepared and the staining should have followed, my head man sent for me to come to the shop, and there hung the figure with its dark green robe with orphreys of *deep blue* and *silver*.

"I thought you'd like to look at it before we stained it," said he.

"STAIN IT!" I said. "I wouldn't touch it; not for sixpence three-farthings!"

There was a sigh of relief all round the shop, and the reply was, "Well, so we all thought!"

Just so; therefore the figure remained, and so was erected in its place. Now suppose I had had men who did what they were told, instead of being encouraged to think and feel and suggest?

A serious word to you about this question of staining. It is a resource very easily open to abuse—to excess. Be careful of the danger, and never stain without first trying the effect on the back of the easel-plate with pure gamboge, and if you wish for a very clear orange-stain, mix with the gamboge a little ordinary red ink. It is too much the custom to "pick out" every bit of silver "canopy" work with dottings and stripings of yellow. A *little* sometimes warms up pleasantly what would be too cold—and the old men used it with effect: but the modern tendency, as is the case in all things merely imitative, is to overdo it. For the old men used it very differently from those who copy them in the way I am speaking of, and, to begin with, used it chiefly on *pure white glass*. Much modern canopy work is done on greenish-white, upon which the stain immediately becomes that greenish-yellow that I have called "brassy." A little of this can be borne, when side by side with it is placed stain upon pure white. The reader will easily find, if he looks for them, plenty of examples in old glass, where the stain upon the white glass has taken even a *rosy* tinge exactly like that of a yellow crocus seen through its white sheath. It is perhaps owing partly to patina on the old glass, which "scumbles" it; but I have myself sometimes succeeded in getting the same >effect by using yellow-stain on pure white glass. A whole window, where the highest light is a greenish white, is to me very unpleasant, and when in addition yellow-stain is used, unbearable. This became a fashion in stained-glass when red-lead-coloured pigments, started by Barff's formula, came into general use. They could not be used on pure white glass, and therefore pure white glass was discarded and greenish-white used instead. I can only say that if the practice of stained-glass were presented to me with this condition—of abstaining from the use of pure white—I would try to learn some useful trade.

There is another question of ideals in the treatment of colour in stained-glass about which a word must be said.

Those who are enthusiastic about the material of stained-glass and its improvement are apt to condemn the degree of heaviness with which windows are ordinarily painted, and this to some extent is a just criticism. But I cannot go the length of thinking that all matt-painting should be avoided, and outline only used; or that stained-glass material can, except under very unusual conditions and in exceptional situations, be independent of this resource. As to the slab-glasses— "Early-English," "Norman," or "stamped-circles"—which are chiefly affected by this question, the texture and surface upon which their special character depends is sometimes a very useful resource in work seen against, or partly against, background of trees or buildings; while against an entirely "borrowed" light perhaps, sometimes, it can almost dispense with any painting. The grey shadows that come from the background play about in the glass and modify its tones, doing the work of painting, and doing it much more beautifully. But this advantage cannot always be had, for it vanishes against clear sky. It is all, therefore, a question of situation and of aspect, and I believe the right rule to be to do in all cases what seems best for every individual bit of glass—that each piece should be "cared for" on its merits and "nursed," so to speak, and its qualities brought out and its beauty heightened by any and every means, just as if it were a jewel to be cut (or left uncut) or foiled (or left unfoiled)—as Benvenuto Cellini would treat, as he tells you he *did* treat, precious stones. There is a fashion now of thinking that gems should be uncut. Well, gems are hardly a fair comparison in discussing stained-glass; for in glass what we aim at is the effect of a composition and combination of a multitude of things, while gems are individual things, for the most part, to be looked at separately. But I would not lay down a rule even about gems. Certainly the universal, awkward, faceting of all precious stones—which is a relic of the mid-Victorian period—is a vulgarity that one is glad to be rid of; but if one *wants* for any reason the special sparkle, here or there, which comes from it, why not use it? I would use it in *stained-glass*—have done so. If I have got my window already brilliant and the whites pure white, and still want, over and above all this, my "Star of the Nativity," let us say, to sparkle out with a light that cannot be its own, shall I not use a faceted "jewel" of glass, forty feet from the eye, where none can see what it is but only what it does, just because it would be a gross vulgarity to use it where it would pretend to be a diamond?

The safe guide (as far as there can be a *guide* where I have maintained that there should not be a *rule*) is, surely, to generally get the depth of colour that you want by the glass itself, *if you can*, and therefore with that aim to deal with rich, full-coloured glass and to promote its manufacture. But this being once done and the resource carried to its full limit, there is no reason why you should deny yourself the further resource of touching it with pigment to any extent that may seem fit to you as an artist, and necessary to get the effect of colour and texture that you are aiming at, in the thing seen as a whole. As to the exaggeration of making accidental streaks in the glass do duty for folds of drapery, and manufacturing glass (as has been done) to meet this purpose, I hold the thing to be a gross degradation and an entire misconception of the relation of materials to art. You may also lay this to mind, as a thing worthy of consideration, that all old glass was painted, and that no school of stained-glass has ever existed which made a principle of refusing this aid. I would never argue from this that such cannot exist, but it is a thing to be thought on.

Throw your net, then, into every sea, and catch what you can. Learn what purple is, in the north ambulatory at York; what green is, in the east window of the same, in the ante-chapel of New College, Oxford, and in the "Adam and Eve" window in the north aisle at Fairford; what blue and red are, in the glorious east window of the nave at Gloucester, and in the glow and gloom of Chartres and Canterbury and King's College, Cambridge. And when you have got all these things in your mind, and gathered lavishly in the field of Nature also, face your problem with a heart heated through with the memory of them all, and with a will braced as to a great and arduous task, but one of rich reward. For remember this (and so let us draw to an end), that in any large window the spaces are so great and the problems so numerous that a *few* colours and groupings of colour, however well chosen, will not suffice. Set out the main scheme of colours first: those that shall lead and preponderate and convey your meaning to the mind and your intended impression to the eye. But if you stop here, the effect will be hard and coarse and cold-hearted in its harmonies, a lot of banging notes like a band all brass, not out of tune perhaps, but craving for the infinite embroidery of the strings and wood.

When, therefore, the main relations of colour have been all set out and decided for your window, turn your attention to *small* differences, to harmonies *round* the harmonies. Make each note into a chord, each tint into a group of tints, not only the strong and bold, but also the subtle and tender; do not miss the value of small modifications of tint that soften brilliance into glow. Study how Nature does it on the petals of the pansy or sweet-pea. You think a pansy is purple, and there an end? but cut out the pale yellow band, the orange central spot, the faint lilacs and whites in between, and where is your pansy gone?

And here I must now leave it to you. But one last little hint, and do not smile at its simplicity.

For the problem, after all, when you have gathered all the hints you can from nature or the past, and collected your resources from however varied fields, resolves itself at last into one question—"*How shall I do it in glass?*" And the practical solving of this problem is in the handling of the actual bits of coloured glass which are the tools of your craft. And for manipulating these I have found nothing so good as that old-fashioned toy—still my own delight when a sick-bed enforces idleness—the kaleidoscope. A sixpenny one, pulled to pieces, will give you the knowledge of how to make it; and you will find a "Bath-Oliver" biscuit-tin, or a large-sized millboard "postal-roll" will make an excellent instrument. But the former is best, because you also then have the lid and the end. If you cut away all the end of the lid except a rim of one-eighth of an inch, and insert in its place with cement a piece of ground-glass, and then, inside this, have another lid of clear glass cemented on to a rim of wood or millboard, you can, in the space between the two, place chips of the glasses you think of using; and, replacing the whole on the instrument, a few minutes of turning with the hand will give you, not hundreds, but thousand of changes, both of the arrangement, and, what is far more important, of the *proportions* of the various colours. You can thus in a few moments watch them pass through an almost infinite succession of changes in their relation to each other, and form your judgment on those changes, choosing finally that which seems best. And I really think that the fact of these combinations being presented to us, as they are by the action of the instrument, arranged in ordered shapes, is a help to the judgment in deciding on the harmonies of colour. It is natural that it should be so. "Order is Heaven's first law." And it is right that we should rejoice in things ordered and arranged, as the savage in his string of beads, and reasonable that we should find it easier to judge them in order rather than confused.

Each in his place. How good a thing it is! how much to be desired! how well if we ourselves could be so, and know of the pattern that we make! For our lives are like the broken bits of glass, sadly or brightly coloured, jostled about and shaken hither and thither, in a seeming confusion, which yet we hope is somewhere held up to a light in which each one meets with his own, and holds his place; and, to the Eye that watches, plays his part in a universal harmony by us, as yet, unseen.

CHAPTER XVII

OF ARCHITECTURAL FITNESS

Come, in thought, reader, and stand in quiet village churches, nestling amongst trees where rooks are building; or in gaps of the chalk downs, where the village shelters from the wind; or in stately cathedrals, where the aisles echo to the footstep and the sound of the chimes comes down, with the memory of the centuries which have lived and died. Here the old artists set their handmark to live now they are gone, and we who see it today see, if our eye be single, with what sincerity they built, carved, or painted their heart and life into these stones. In such a spirit and for such a memorial you too must do your work, to be weighed by the judgment of the coming ages, when you in turn are gone, in the same balance as theirs—perhaps even side by side with it.

And will you dare to venture? Have no fear if you also bring your best. But if we enter on work like this as to a mere market for our wares, and with no other thought than to make a brisk business with those that buy and sell; we well may pray that some merciful scourge of small cords drive us also hence to dig or beg (which is more honourable), lest worse befall us!

And I do not say these things because this or that place is "God's house." All places are so, and the first that was called so was the bare hillside; but because you are a man and have indeed here arrived, as there the lonely traveller did, at the arena of your wrestling. But, granted that you mean to hold your own and put your strength into it, I have brought you to these grave walls to consult with them as to the limits they impose upon your working.

And perhaps the most important of all is already observed by your *being* here, for it is important that you should visit, whenever possible, the place where you are to do work; if you are not able to do this, get all the particulars you can as to aspect and surroundings. And yet a reservation must be made, even upon all this; for everything depends upon the way we use it, and if you only have an eye to the showing off of your work to advantage, treating the church as a mere frame for your picture, it would be better that your window should misfit and have to be cut down and altered, or anything else happen to it that would help to put it back and make it take second place. It is so hard to explain these things so that they cannot be misconstrued; but you remember I quoted the windows at St. Philip's, Birmingham, as an example of noble thought and work carried to the pitch of perfection and design. But that was in a classic building, with large, plain, single openings without tracery. Do you think the artist would have let himself go, in that full and ample way, in a beautiful Gothic building full of lovely architectural detail? Not so: rather would he have made his pictures hang lightly and daintily in the air amongst the slender shafts, as in St. Martin's Church in the same town, at Jesus College and at All Saints' Church, Cambridge, at Tamworth; and in Lyndhurst, and many another church where the architecture, to say truth, had but slender claims to such respect.

In short, you must think of the building first, and make your windows help it. You must observe its scale and the spacing and proportions of its style, and place your own work, with whatever new feeling and new detail may be natural to you, well within those circumscribing bounds.

But here we find ourselves suddenly brought sharp up, face to face with a most difficult and thorny subject, upon which we have rushed without knowing it. "Must we observe then" (you say) "the style of the building into which we put our work, and not have a style of our own that is native to us"?

"This is contrary to all you have been preaching! The old men did not so. Did they not add the fancies of their own time to the old work, and fill with their dainty, branching tracery the severe, round-headed, Norman openings of Peterborough and Gloucester? Did fifteenth-century men do thirteenth-century glass when they had to refill a window of that date?" No. Nor must you. Never imitate, but graft your own work on to the old, reverently, and only changing from it so far forth as you, like itself, have also a living tradition, springing from mastery of craft—naturally, spontaneously, and inevitably.

Whether we shall ever again have such a tradition running throughout all the arts is a thing that cannot possibly be foretold. But three things we may be quite sure of.

First, that if it comes it will not be by way of any imitative revival of a past style;

Second, that it will be in harmony with the principles of Nature; and

Third, that it will be founded upon the crafts, and brought about by craftsmen working in it with their own hands, on the materials of architecture, designing only what they themselves can execute, and giving employment to others only in what they themselves can do.

A word about each of these three conditions.

In the course of the various attempted revivals in architecture that have taken place during the past sixty years, it has been frequently urged both by writers and architects that we should agree to revive some *one* style of ancient art that might again become a national style of architecture. It would, indeed, no doubt be better, if we must speak in a dead language, to agree to use only one, instead of our present confusion of tongues: but what, after all, is the adopting of this principle at all but to engage once again in the replanting of a full-grown tree— the mistake of the Renaissance and the Gothic revival repeated? Such things never take firm root or establish healthy growth which lives and goes on of its own vitality. They never succeed in obtaining a natural, national sympathy and acceptance. The movement is a scholarly and academic one, and the art so remains. The reaction against it is always a return to materials, and almost always the first result of this is a revival of simplicity. People get tired of being surrounded with elaborate mouldings and traceries and other architectural features, which are not the natural growth of their own day but of another day long since dead, which had other thoughts and moods, feelings and aspirations. "Let us have straightforward masonry and simple openings, and ornament them with something from Nature."

So in the very midst of the pampered and enervated over-refinement of Roman decay, Constantine did something more than merely turn the conquering eagle back, against the course of the heavens, for which Dante seems to blame him, when he established his capital at Byzantium; for there at once upon the new soil, and in less than a single century, sprang to life again all the natural modes of building and decoration that, despised as barbaric, had been ignored and forgotten amid the Roman luxury and sham.

It is a curious feature of these latest days of ours that this searching after sincerity should seem to be leading us towards a similar revival; taking even very much the same forms. We went back, at the time of the Gothic revival, to the forgotten Gothic art of stained-glass; now tired, as it would seem, of the insincerity and mere spirit of imitation with which it and similar arts have been practised, a number of us appear to be ready to throw it aside, along with scholarly mouldings and traceries, and build our arts afresh out of the ground, as was done by the Byzantines, with plain brickwork, mosaic, and matched slabs of marble. Definite examples in recent architecture will occur to the reader. But I am thinking less of these—which for the most part are deliberate and scholastic revivals of a particular style, founded on the study of previous examples and executed on rigid academic methods—than of what appears to be a widespread awakening to principles of simplicity, sincerity, and common sense in the arts of building generally. Signs are not wanting of a revived interest in building—a revived interest in materials for their own sake, and a revived practice of personally working in them and experimenting with them. One calls to mind examples of these things, growing in number daily—plain and strong furniture made with the designer's own hands and without machinery, and enjoyed in the making—made for actual places and personal needs and tastes; houses built in the same spirit by architects who condescend to be masons also; an effort here and an effort there to revive the common ways of building that used to prevail—and not so long ago—for the ordinary housing and uses of country-folk and country-life, and which gave us cottages, barns, and sheds throughout the length and breadth of the land; simple things for simple needs, built by simple men, without self-consciousness, for actual use and pleasant dwelling; traditional construction and the habits of making belonging to the country-side. These still linger in the time-honoured ways of making the waggon and the cart and the plough; but they have vanished from architecture and building except in so far as they are being now, as I have said, consciously and deliberately revived by men who are going back from academic methods, to found their arts once more upon the actual making of things with their own hand and as their hand and materials will guide them.

This was what happened in the time to which I have referred: in the dawn of the Christian era and of a new civilisation; and it has special interest for us of today, because it was not a case of an infant or savage race, beginning all things from seed; but the revival, as in Sparta, centuries before it, of simplicity and sincerity of life, in the midst of enervation, luxury, and decay.

This seems our hope for the future.

There has already gathered together in the great field of the arts of today a little Byzantium of the crafts setting itself to learn from the beginning how things are actually made, how built, hammered, painted, cut, stitched; casting aside theories and academical thought, and founding itself upon simplicity, and sincerity, and materials. And the architect who condescends, or, as we should rather say, aspires, to be a >builder and a master-mason, true director of his craft, will, if things go on as they seem now going, find in the near future a band around him of other workers so minded, and will have these bright tools of the accessory crafts ready to his hand. This it is, if anything, that will solve all the vexed questions of "style," and lead, if anything will, to the art of the times to be. For the reason why the nineteenth century complained so constantly that it had "no style of architecture" was surely because it had *every* style of architecture, and a race of architects who could design in every style because they could build in no style; knew by practical handling and tooling nothing of the real natures and capacities of stone or brick or wood or glass; received no criticism from their materials; whereas these should have daily and hourly moulded their work and formed the very breath of its life, warning and forbidding on the one hand, suggesting on the other, and so directing over all.

I have thought fit, dear student, to touch on these great questions in passing, that you may know where you stand; but our real business is with ourselves: to make ourselves so secure upon firm standing ground, in our own particular province, that when the hour arrives, it may find in us the man. Let us therefore return again from these bright hopes to consider those particular details of architectural fitness which are our proper business as workers in glass.

What, then, in detail, are the rules that must guide us in placing windows in ancient buildings? But first—*may* we place windows in ancient buildings at all? "No," say some; "because we have no right to touch the past; it is 'restoration,' a word that has covered, in the past," they say (and we must agree with them), "a mass of artistic crime never to be expiated, and of loss never to be repaired." "Yes," say others, "because new churches will be older in half-an-hour—half-an-hour older; for the world has moved, and where will you draw the line? Also, glass has *to be renewed*, you must put in something, or some one must."

Let each decide the question for himself; but, supposing you admit that it is permissible, what are the proper restrictions and conditions?

You must not tell a lie, or "match" old work, joining your own on to it as if itself were old.

Shall we work in the style of the "New art," then—"*l'art Nouveau*"? the style of the last new poster? the art-tree, the art-bird, the art-squirm, and the ace of spades form of ornament?

Heaven in mercy defend us and forbid it!

Canopies are venerable; thirteenth-century panels and borders are venerable, the great traditional vestments are so, and liturgy, and symbolism, and ceremony. These are not things of one age alone, but belong to all time. Get, wherever possible, authority on all these points.

Must we work in a "style," then—a "Gothic" style?

No.

What rule, then?

It is hard to formulate so as to cover all questions, but something thus:—

Take forms, and proportions, and scale from the style of the church you are to work in.

Add your own feeling to it from—

(1) The feeling of the day, but the best and most reverent feeling.

(2) From Nature.

(3) From (and the whole conditioned by) materials and the knowledge of craft.

Finally, let us say that you must consider each case on its merits, and be ready even sometimes perhaps to admit that the old white glass may be better for a certain position than your new glass could be, while old *stained-glass*, of course, should always be sacred to you, a thing to be left untouched. Even where new work seems justifiable and to be demanded, proceed as if treading on holy ground. Do not try crude experiments on venerable and beautiful buildings, but be modest and reticent; know the styles of the past thoroughly and add your own fresh feeling to them reverently. And in thought do not think it necessary to be novel in order to be original. There is quite enough originality in making a noble figure of a saint, or treating with reverent and dignified art some actual theme of Scripture or tradition, and working into its detail the sweetness of nature and the skill of your hands, without going into eccentricity for the sake of novelty, and into weak allegory to show your originality and independence, tired with the world-old truths and laws of holy life and noble character. And this leads us to the point where we must speak of these deep things in the great province of thought.

CHAPTER XVIII

OF THOUGHT, IMAGINATION, AND ALLEGORY

"The first thing one should demand of a man who calls himself an artist is that he has something to say, some truth to teach, some lesson to enforce. Don't you think so?"

Thus once said to me an artist of respectable attainment.

"I don't care a hang for subject; give me good colour, composition, fine effects of light, skill in technique, that's all one wants. Don't you think so?"

Thus once said to me a member of a window-committee, himself also an artist.

To both I answered, and would answer with all the emphasis possible—No!

The *first* duty of an artist, as of every other kind of worker, is to know his business; and, unless he knows it, all the "truths" he wishes to "teach," and the lessons he wishes to enforce, are but degraded and discredited in the eyes of men by his bungling advocacy.

On the other hand, the artist who has trained himself to speak with the tongues of angels and after all has nothing to say, is also, to me, an imperfect being. What follows is written, as the whole book is written, for the young student, just beginning his career and feeling the pressure and conflict of these questions. For such I must venture to discuss points which the wise and the experienced may pass by.

The present day is deluged with allegory; and the first thing three students out of four wish to attempt when they arrive at the stage of original art is the presentation, by figures and emblems, of some deep abstract truth, some problem of the great battle of life, some force of the universe that they begin to feel around them, pressing upon their being. Forty years ago such a thing was hardly heard of. In the sketching-clubs at the Academies of that day, the historical, the concrete, or the respectably pious were all that one ever saw. We can hardly realise it, the art of the late sixties. The pre-Raphaelite brotherhood, as such, a thing of the past, and seemingly leaving few imitators. Burne-Jones just heard of as a strange, unknown artist, who wouldn't exhibit his pictures, but who had done some queer new kind of stained-glass windows at Lyndhurst, which one might perhaps be curious to see when we went (as of course we must) to worship "Leighton's great altar-piece." Nay, ten years later, at the opening of the Grosvenor Gallery, the new, imaginative, and allegorical art could be met with a large measure of derision, and *Punch* could write, regarding it, an audacious and contemptuous parody of the "Palace of Art"; while, abroad, Botticelli's *Primavera* hung over a door, and the attendants at the *Uffizii* were puzzled by requests, granted grudgingly (*if* granted), to have his other pictures placed for copying and study! Times have altogether changed, and we now see in every school competition—often set as the subject of such—abstract and allegorical themes, demanding for their adequate expression the highest and deepest thought and the noblest mood of mind and views of life.

It is impossible to lay down any hard and fast rule about these things, for each case must differ. There is such a thing as *genius*, and where that is there is but small question of rules or even of youth or age, maturity or immaturity. And even apart from the question of genius the mind of childhood is a very precious thing, and "the thoughts of youth are long, long thoughts." Nay, the mere *fact* of youth with its trials, is a great thing; we shall never again have such a chance, such fresh, responsive hearts, such capacity for feeling—for suffering—that school of wisdom and source of inspiration! It is well to record its lessons while they are fresh, to jot down for ourselves, if we can, something of the passing hours; to store up their thoughts and feelings for future expression perhaps, when our powers of expression have grown more worthy of them; but it is not well to try to make universal lessons out of, or universal applications of, what we haven't ourselves learned. Our own proper lesson at this time is to learn our trade; to strengthen our weak hands and train the ignorance of our mind to knowledge day by day, strenuously, and only *spurred on by* the deep stirrings of thought and life within us, which generally ought to remain for the present *unspoken*.

A great point of happiness in this dangerous and critical time is to have a definite trade; learnt in its completeness and practised day by day, step by step, upwards from its elements, in constant subservience to wise and kind mastership. This indeed is a golden lot, and one rare in these days; and perhaps we must not look to be so shielded. This was the sober and happy craftsmanship of the Middle Ages, and produced for us all that imagery and ornature, instinct with gaiety and simplicity of heart, which decorates, where the hand of the ruthless restorer has spared it, the churches and cathedrals of Europe.

But in these changeful days it would be rash indeed to forecast where lies the sphere of duty for any individual life. It may lie in the reconstruction by solitary, personal experiment, of some forgotten art or system, the quiet laying of foundation for the future rather than building the monument of today. Or perhaps the self-devoted life of the seer may be the Age's chief need, and it is not a Giotto that is wanted for the twentieth century but a Dante or a Blake, with the accompanying destiny of having to prove as they did—

> "si come sa di sale
> Lo pane altrui, e com'h duro calle
> Lo scendere e'l salir per l'altrui scale."

> "how tastes of salt
> The bread of others, and how is hard the passage
> To go down and to go up by other's stairs."
> —*Paradise*, xvii. 58.

But, however these things be, whether working happily in harmony with the scheme of things around us, and only concerned to give it full expression, or not;

whether we are the fortunate apprentices of a well-taught trade, gaining secure and advancing knowledge day by day, or whether we are lonely experimentalists, wringing the secret from reluctant Nature and Art upon some untrodden path; there is one last great principle that covers all conditions, solves all questions, and is an abiding rock which remains, unfailing foundation on which all may build; and that is the constant measuring of our smallness against the greatness of things, a thing which, done in the right spirit, does not daunt, but inspires. For the greatness of all things is ours for the winning, almost for the asking.

The great imaginative poets and thinkers and artists of the mid-nineteenth century have drawn aside for us the curtain of the world behind the veil, and he would be an ambitious man who would expect to set the mark higher, in type of beauty or depth of feeling, than they have placed it for us; but all must hope to do so, even if they do not expect it; for the great themes are not exhausted or ever to be exhausted; and the storehouse of the great thought and action of the past is ever open to us to clothe our nakedness and enrich our poverty; we need only ask to have.

"Ah!" said Coningsby, "I should like to be a great man."

The stranger threw at him a scrutinising glance. His countenance was serious. He said in a voice of almost solemn melody—

"Nurture your mind with great thoughts. To believe in the heroic makes heroes."

All the great thoughts of the world are stored up in books, and all the great books of the world, or nearly all, have been translated into English. You should make it a systematic part of your life to search these things out and, if only by a page or two, try how far they fit your need. We do not enough realise how wide a field this is, how great an undertaking, how completely unattainable except by carefully husbanding our time from the start, how impossible it is in the span of a human life to read the great books unless we strictly save the time which so many spend on the little books. Ruskin's words on this subject, almost harsh in their blunt common sense, bring the matter home so well that I cannot refrain from quoting them.

"Do you know, if you read this, that you cannot read that—that what you lose today you cannot gain to-morrow? Will you go and gossip with your housemaid, or your stable-boy, when you may talk with queens and kings; or flatter yourselves that it is with any worthy consciousness of your own claims to respect that you jostle with the common crowd for entrie here, and audience there, when all the while this eternal court is open to you, with its society wide as the world, multitudinous as its days, the chosen, and the mighty, of every place and time? Into that you may enter always; in that you may take fellowship and rank according to your wish; from that, once entered into it, you can never be outcast but by your own fault; by your aristocracy of companionship there, your own inherent aristocracy will be assuredly tested, and the motives with which you strive to take high place in the society of the living, measured, as to all the truth and sincerity that are in them, by the place you desire to take in this company of the Dead."

This is the great world of BOOKS that is open to you; and how shall you find your way in it, in these days, amongst the plethora of the second and third and fourth rate, shouting out at you and besieging your attention on every stall? It is no more possible to give you entire guidance towards this than to give complete advice on any other problem of life; your own nature must be your guide, choosing the good and refusing the evil in the degree in which itself is good or evil. But one may name some landmarks, set up some guide-posts, and the best of all guidance surely is not that of a guide-post, but that of a guide, a kindly hand of one who knows the way, to take your hand.

Do you ask for such a guide? A man of our own day, in full view of all its questions from the loftiest to the least, and heart and soul engaged in them, with deep and sympathetic wisdom born of his own companionship with all the great thoughts of the ages? One surely need not hesitate a moment in naming as the one for our special needs the writer we have just quoted.

Scattered up and down the whole of his works is constant reference to and commentary upon the great themes of all ages, the great creeds of all peoples.

"Queen of the Air," "Aratra Pentelici," "Ariadne Florentina," "The Mornings in Florence," "St. Mark's Rest," "The Oxford Inaugural Lectures," "The Bible of Amiens," "Fors Clavigera."

With these as portals you can enter by easy steps into the whole universe of great things: the divine myth and symbolism of the old pagan world (as we call it) and of more recent Christendom; all the makers of ancient Greece and Italy and of our own England; worship and kingship and leadership, and the high thought and noble deed of all times. And clustering in groups round these centres is the world of books. All Theology, Philosophy, Poetry, Sacred History; Homer, Plato, Virgil, the Bible, and the Breviary. The great doctors and saints, kings and heroes, poets and painters, Gerome and Dominic and Francis; St. Louis and C[œ]ur-de-Lion; Dante, St. Jerome, Chaucer, and Froissart; Botticelli, Giotto, Angelico; the "Golden Legend"; and many another ancient or modern legend and story or passage from the history of some great and splendid life, or illuminating hint upon the beauties of liturgy and symbolism. They, and a hundred other things, are all gathered up and introduced to us in Ruskin's books; and we are shown them from the exact standpoint from which they are most likely to appeal to us, and be of use. There never was a great world made so easy and pleasant of entrance for the adventuring traveller; you have only to enter and take possession.

Do you incline towards myth and symbolism and allegory—the expression of abstract thought by beautiful figures? Read the myths of Greece expounded to you in their exquisite spirituality in the "Queen of the Air." Or is your bent devotion and the devout life, expressed in thrilling story and gorgeous colour? Read, say, the life of St. Catherine or of St. George in the "Golden Legend." Or are you in love, and would express its spring-time beauty? Translate into your own native language of form and colour "The Romaunt of the Rose."

For the great safeguard and guide in the perilous forest of fancy is to find enough interest in the actual facts of some history or the qualities of some heroic character, whether real or fabled, round which at first you may group your thought and allegory. Listen to *them*, and try to formulate and illustrate *their* meaning, not to announce your own. Do not set puzzles, or set things that will be puzzling, without the highest and deepest reasons and the apostleship urgently laid upon you so to do—but let your allegory surround some definite subject, so that men in general can see it and say, "Yes, that is so and so," and go away satisfied rather than puzzled and affronted; leaving the inner few for whom you really speak, the hearts that, you hope, are waiting for your message, to find it out (and you need have no fear that they will do so), and to say, "Yes, that *means* so and so, and it is a good thought."

For, remember always that, even if you conceive that you have a mission laid upon you to declare Truth, it is most sternly conditioned by an obligation, as binding as itself and of as high authority, to set forth Beauty: the holiness of beauty equally with the beauty of holiness. No amount of good intent can make up for lack of skill; it is your business to know your business. Youth always would begin with allegory, but the ambition of the good intention is generally in exactly the reverse proportion to the ability to carry it out in expression. But the true allegory that appeals to all is the presentment of noble natures and of noble deeds. Where, for most people at any rate, is the "allegory" in the Theseus or the Venus of Milo? Yet is not the whole race of man the better for them?

Work, therefore, quietly and continually at the great themes ready set for you in the story of the past and "understanded of the people," while you are patiently strengthening and maturing your powers of art in safety, sheltered from yourself, and sheltered from the condemnation due to the too presumptuous assumption of apostleship. For it is one thing to stand forth and say, "*I* have a message to deliver to the world," and quite another to say, "*There is* such a message, and it has fallen to me to be its mouthpiece; woe is me, because I am a man of unclean lips." It is needless, therefore—nay, it is harmful—to be always breaking your heart against tasks beyond your strength. Work in some little province; get foothold and grow outwards from it; go on from weakness to strength, and then from strength to the stronger, doing the things you *can* do while you practise towards the things you hope to do, and illustrating impersonal themes until the time comes for you to try your own individual battle in the great world of thought and feeling; till, mature in strength equal to the portrayal of great natures, the Angels of God as shown forth by you may be recognised as indeed Spirit, and His Ministers as flaming Fire.

There is even yet one last word, and that is, in all the *minor* symbolism surrounding your subjects, to observe a due proportion. For you may easily be tempted to allow some beautiful little fancy, not essential to the subject, to find expression in a form or symbol that will thrust itself unduly on the attention, and will only puzzle and distract.

Never let little things come first, and never let them be allowed at all to the damage, or impairing, or obscuring of the simplicity and dignity of the great things; remembering always that the first function of a window is to have stately and seemly figures in beautiful glass, and not to arrest or distract the attention of the spectator with puzzles. Given the great themes adequately expressed, the little fancies may then cluster round them and will be carried lightly, as the victor wears his wreath; while, on the other hand, if these be lacking no amount of symbolism or attribute will supply their place. "*Cucullus non facit monachum*," as the old proverb says—"It is not the hood that makes the monk," but the ascetic face you depict within it. Indeed, rather beware of trusting even to the ordinary, well-recognised symbols in common use, and being misled by them to think you have done something you have not done; and rather withhold these until the other be made sure. Get your figures dignified and your faces beautiful; show the majesty or the sanctity that you are aiming at in these alone, and your saint will be recognised as saintly without his halo of glory, and your angel as angelic without his tongue of flame.

In my own practice, when drawing from the life, I make a great point of keeping back all these ornaments and symbols of attribute, until I feel that my figure alone expresses itself fully, as far as my powers go, without them. No ornament upon the robe, or the crosier, or the sword; above all, no circle round the head, until—the figure standing out at last and seeming to represent, as near as may be, the true pastor or warrior it claims to represent—the moment arrives when I say, "Yes, I have done all I can,—*now* he may have his nimbus!"

CHAPTER XIX

Of General Conduct and Procedure—Amount of Legitimate Assistance—The Ordinary Practice—The Great Rule—The Second Great Rule—Four Things to Observe—Art v. Routine—The Truth of the Case—The Penalty of Virtue in the Matter—The Compensating Privilege—Practical Applications—An Economy of Time in the Studio—Industry—Work "To Order"—Clients and Patrons—And Requests Reasonable and Unreasonable—The Chief Difficulty the Chief Opportunity—But ascertain all Conditions before starting Work—Business Habits—Order—Accuracy—Setting out Cartoon Forms—An Artist must Dream—But Wake—Three Plain Rules.

Having now described, as well as I can, the whole of your equipment—of hand, and head, and heart—your mental and technical weapons for the practice of stained-glass, there now follow a few simple hints to guide you in the use of them; how best to dispose your forces, and on what to employ them. This must be a very broken and fragmentary chapter, full of little everyday matters, very different to the high themes we have just been trying to discuss—and relating chiefly to your conduct of the thing as a business, and your relationships with the interests that surround you; modes of procedure, business hints, practical matters. I am sorry, just as you were beginning (I hope) to be warmed to the subject, and fired with the high ambitions that it suggests, to take and toss you into the cold world of matter-of-fact things; but that is life, and we have to face it. Open the door into the cold air and let us bang at it straight away!

Now there is one great and plain question that contains all the rest; you do not see it now, but you will find it facing you before you have gone very far. The great question, "Must I do it all myself, or may I train pupils and assistants?"

Let us first amplify the question and get it fairly and fully stated. Then we shall have a better chance of being able to answer it wisely.

I have described or implied elsewhere the usual practice in the matter amongst those who produce stained-glass on a large scale. In great establishments the work is divided up into branches: designers, cartoonists, painters, cutters, lead workers, kiln-men: none of whom, as a rule, know any branch of the work except their own.

Obviously one of the principal contentions of this book is against the idea that such division, as practised, is an ideal method.

On the other hand, you will gather that the writer himself uses the service of assistants.

While in the plates at the end are examples of glass where everything has been done by the artists themselves (Plates I., II., III., IV., VII.).

I must freely confess that when I first saw in the work of these men the beauty resulting from the personal touch of the artist on the whole of the cutting and leading, a qualm of doubt arose whether the practice of admitting *any* other hand to my assistance was not a compromise to some extent with absolute ideal; whether it were not the only right plan, after all, to do the whole oneself; to sit down to the bench with one's drawing, and pick out the glass, piece by piece, on its merits, carefully considering each bit as it passed through hand; cutting it and trimming it affectionately to preserve its beauties, and, later, leading it into its place with thicker or thinner lead, in the same careful spirit. But I do not think so. I fancy the truth to be that the *whole* business should be opened up to all, and afterwards each should gravitate to his place by natural fitness. For the cartoonist *once having the whole craft* requires more constant practice in drawing to keep himself a good cartoonist than he would get if he also did all the other work of each window; quantity being in this matter even essential to quality. I think we must look for more monumental figures, achieved by the delegation of minor craft matters, in short, by co-operation. Nevertheless, I have never felt less certainty in pronouncing on any question of my craft than in this particular matter; whether, to get the best attainable results, one should do the whole of the work oneself. On the other hand, I never felt *more* certainty in pronouncing on any question of the craft, than now in laying down as an absolute rule and condition of doing good work at all: that one should be *able* to do the whole of the work oneself. *That* is the key to the whole situation, but it is not the whole key; for following close upon it comes the rule that springs naturally out of it; that, being a master oneself, one must make it one's object to train all assistants towards mastership also: to give them the whole ladder to climb. This at least has been the case with the work of my own which is shown in the other collotypes. There has been assistance, but every one of those assisting has had the opportunity to learn to make, and according to the degree of his talent is actually able to make, the whole of a stained-glass window himself. There is not a touch of painting on any of the panels shown which is not by a hand that can also cut and lead and design and draw, and perform all the other offices pertaining to stained-glass noted in the foregoing pages.

Speaking generally, I care not whether a man calls himself Brown, or Brown and Co., or, co-operating with others, works under the style of Brown, Jones and Robinson, so long as he observe four things.

(1) Not to direct what he cannot practise;

(2) To make masters of apprentices, or aim at making them;

(3) To keep his hand of mastery over the whole work personally at all stages; and

(4) To be prepared sometimes to make sacrifices of profit for the sake of the Art, should the interests of the two clash.

Such an one we must call an artist, a master, and a worthy craftsman. It is almost impossible to describe the deadening influence which a routine embodying the reverse of these four things has upon the mind of those who should be artists. Under this influence not only is the subdivision of labour which places each successive operation in separate hands accepted as a matter of course, but into each operation itself this separation imports a spirit of lassitude and dullness and compliance with false conditions and limited aims which would seem almost incredible in those practising what should be an inspiring art. To men so trained, so employed, all counsels of perfection are foolishness; all idea of tentative work, experiment, modification while in progress, is looked upon as mere delusion. To them work consists of a series of never-varied formulas, all fitting into each other and combined to aim at producing a definite result, the like of which they have produced a thousand times before and will produce a thousand times again.

"With us," once said, to a friend of the writer, a man so trained, "it's a matter of judgment and experience. It's all nonsense this talk about seeing work at a distance and against the sky, and so forth, while as to the ever taking it down again for retouching after once erecting it, that could only be done by an amateur. We paint a good deal of the work on the bench, and never see it as a whole until it's leaded up; but then we know what we want and get it."

"We know what we want!" To what a pass have we come that such a thing could be spoken by any one engaged in the arts! Were it wholly and universally true, nothing more would be needed in condemnation of wide fields of modern practice in the architectural and applied arts, for, most assuredly it is a sentence that could never be spoken of any one worthy of the name of artist that ever lived. Whence would you like instances quoted? Literature? Painting? Sculpture? Music? Their name is legion in the history of all these arts, and in the lives of the great men who wrought in them.

For a taste—

Did Michael Angelo "know what he wanted" when, half-way through his figure, he found the block not large enough, and had to make the limb too short?

Did Beethoven know, when he evolved a movement in one of his concerted pieces out of a quarrel with his landlady? and another, "from singing or rather roaring up and down the scale," until at last he said, "I think I have found a motive"—as one of his biographers relates? Tennyson, when he corrected and re-corrected his poems from youth to his death? Dürer, the precise, the perfect, able to say, "It cannot be better done," yet re-engraving a portion of his best-known plate, and frankly leaving the rejected portion half erased? Titian, whose custom it was to lay aside his pictures for long periods and then criticise them, imagining that he was looking at them "with the eyes of his worst enemy"?

There is not, I suppose, in the English language a more "perfect" poem than "Lycidas." It purports to have been written in a single day, and its wholeness and unity and crystalline completeness give good colour to the thought that it probably was so.

"Thus sang the uncouth swain to the oaks and rills,
While the still morn went out with sandals gray;
He touched the tender stops of various quills,
With eager thought warbling his Doric lay:

And now the sun had stretched out all the hills,
And now was dropt into the western bay:
At last he rose, and twitched his mantle blue;
To-morrow, to fresh woods and pastures new."

Yet, regarding it, the delightful Charles Lamb writes:—

"I had thought of the *Lycidas* as of a full-grown beauty,—as springing with all its parts absolute,—till, in evil hour, I was shown the original copy of it, together with the other minor poems of its author, in the library of Trinity, kept like something to be proud of. I wish they had thrown them in the Cam, or sent them, after the later cantos of Spenser, into the Irish Channel. How it staggered me to see the fine things in their ore!—interlined, corrected, as if their words were mortal, alterable, displaceable at pleasure; as if they might have been otherwise, and just as good; as if inspiration were made up of parts, and those fluctuating, successive, indifferent! I will never go into the workshop of any great artist again, nor desire a sight of his picture, till it is fairly off the easel; no, not if Raphael were to be alive again, and painting another Galatea."

But the real truth of the case is that whatever "inspiration" may be, and whether or not "made up of parts," it, or man's spirit and will in all works of art, has to *deal with* things so made up; and not only so, but also as described by the other words here chosen: *fluctuating, successive,* and *indifferent.* You have to deal with the whole sum of things all at once; the possible material crowds around the artist's will, shifting, changing, presenting at all stages and in all details of a work of art, infinite and continual choice. "Nothing," we are told, "is single," but all things have relations with each other. How much more, then, is it true that every bit of glass in a window is the centre of such relations with its brother and sister pieces, and that nothing is final until all is finished? A work of art is like a battle; conflict after conflict, man[œ]uvre after man[œ]uvre, combination after combination. The general does not pin himself down from the outset to one plan of tactics, but watches the field and moulds its issues to his will, according to the yielding or the resistance of the opposing forces, keeping all things solvent until the combinations of the strife have woven together into a soluble problem, upon which he can launch the final charge that shall bring him back with victory.

So also is all art, and you must hold all things in suspense. Aye! the last touch more or less of light or shade or colour upon the smallest piece, keeping all open and solvent to the last, until the whole thing rushes together and fuses into a harmony. It is not to be done by "judgment and experience," for all things are new, and there are no two tasks the same; and it is impossible for you from the outset to "know what you want," or to know it at any stage until you can say that the whole work is finished.

"But if we work on these methods we shall only get such a small quantity of work done, and it will be so costly done on a system like that you speak of! Make my assistants masters, and so rivals! put a window in, and take it out again, forsooth!" What remedy or answer for this?

Well—setting aside the question of the more or less genius—there are only two solutions that I can see:—an increase in industry or a possible decrease in profit, though much may be accomplished in mitigation of these hard conditions, if they prove *too* hard, by a good and economical system of work, and by time-saving appliances and methods.

But, after all, you were not looking out for an easy task, were you, in this world of stress and strain to have the privileges of an artist's life without its penalties? Why, look you, you must remember that besides the business of "saving your soul," which you may share in common with every one else, *you* have the special privilege of *enjoying for its own sake your personal work in the world.*

And you must expect to pay for that privilege at some corresponding personal cost; all the more so in these days when your lot is so exceptional a fortune, and when to enjoy daily work falls to so few. Nevertheless, when I say "enjoy" I do not mean that art is easy or pleasant in the way that ease is pleasant; there is nothing harder; and the better the artist, probably the harder it is. But you enjoy it because of its privileges; because beauty is delightful; because you know that good art does high and unquestioned service to man, and is even one of the ways for the advancing of the kingdom of God.

That should be pleasure enough for any one, and compensation for any pains. You must learn the secret of human suffering—and you can only learn it by tasting it—because it is yours to point its meaning to others and to give the message of hope.

In this spirit, then, and within these limitations, must you guide your own work and claim the co-operation of others, and arrange your relationships with them, and the limits of their assistance and your whole personal conduct and course of procedure:—

To be yourself a master.

To train others up to mastery.

To keep your hand over the whole.

To work in a spirit of sacrifice.

These things once firmly established, questions of procedure become simple. But a few detached hints may be given. I shall string them together just as they come.

An Economy of Time in the Studio.—Have a portion of your studio or work-room wall lined with thin boarding—"picture-backing" of 1/8 inch thick is enough, and this is to *pin things on to.* The cartoon is what you are busy upon, but you must "think in glass" all the time you are drawing it. Have therefore, pinned up, a number of slips of paper—a foolscap half-sheet divided *vertically* into two long strips I find best.

On these write down every direction to the cutter, or the painter, or the designer of minor ornament, *the moment it comes into your mind,* as you work at the charcoal drawing. If you once let the moment pass you will never remember these things again, but you will have them constantly forced back upon your memory, by the mistranslations of your intention which will face you when you first see your work in the glass. This practice is a huge saving of time—and of disappointment. But you also want this convenient wall space for a dozen other needs; for tracings and shiftings of parts, and all sorts of essays and suggestions for alteration.

That we should work always.—I hope it is not necessary to urge the importance of *work*. It is not of much use to work only when we *feel inclined*; many people very seldom do feel naturally inclined. Perhaps there are few things so sweet as the triumph of working *through* disinclination till it is leavened through with the will and becomes enjoyment by becoming conquest. To work through the dead three o'clock period on a July afternoon with an ache in the small of one's back and one's limbs all a-jerk with nervousness, drooping eyelids, and a general inclination to scream. At such a time, I fear, one sometimes falls back on rather low and sordid motives to act as a spur to the lethargic will. I think of the shortness of the time, the greatness of the task, but also of all those hosts of others who, if I lag, must pass me in the race. Not of actual rivals—or good nature and sense of comradeship would always break the vision—but of possible and unknown ones whom it is my habit to club all together and typify under the style and title of "that fellow Jones." And at such a time it is my habit to say or think, "Aha! I bet Jones is on his back under a plane tree!"—or thoughts to that effect—and grasp the charcoal firmer.

It is habits and dodges and ways of thinking such as these that will gradually cultivate in you the ability to "stand and deliver," as they say in the decorative arts. For, speaking now to the amateur (if any such, picture-painter or student, are hesitating on the brink of an art new to them), you must know that these arts are not like picture-painting, where you can choose your own times and seasons: they are always done to definite order and expected in a definite time; and that brings me to speak of the very important subject of "Clients."

Of Clients and Patrons.—It must, of course, be left to each one to establish his own relations with those who ask work of him; but a few hints may be given.

You will get many requests that will seem to you unreasonable and impossible of carrying out—some no doubt will really be so; but at least *consider them*. Remember what we said a little way back—not to be set on your own allegory, but to accept your subject from outside and add your poetic thought to it. And also what in another place we said about keeping all "solvent"—so do with actual suggestion of subject and with the wishes of your client: treat the whole thing as "raw material," and all surrounding questions as factors in one general problem. Here also Ruskin has a pregnant word of advice—as indeed where has he not?— "A great painter's business is to do what the public ask of him, in the way that shall be helpful and instructive to them." You cannot always do what people ask, but you can do it more often than a headstrong man would at first think.

I was once doing a series of small square panels, set at intervals in the height of some large, tall windows, and containing Scripture subjects, the intermediate spaces being filled with "grisaille" work. The subjects, of course, had to be approximately on one scale, and several of them became very tough problems on account of this restriction. However, all managed to slip through somehow till we came to "Jacob's Ladder," and there I stood firm, or perhaps I ought rather to say *stuck fast.* "How is it possible," I said to my client, "that you can have a picture of the 'Fall' in one panel with Eve's figure taking up almost the whole height of it, and have a similar panel with 'Angels Ascending and Descending' up and down a ladder? There are only two ways of doing it—to put the ladder far off in a landscape, which would reduce it to insignificance, and besides be unsuitable in glass; or to make the angels the size of dolls. Don't you see that it's impossible?" No, he didn't see that it was impossible. What he wanted was "Jacob's Ladder"; the possibility or otherwise was nothing to him. He said (what you'll often hear said, reader, if you do stained-glass), "I don't, of course, know anything about art, and I can't say how this could be done; that is the artist's province."

It was in my younger days, and I'm afraid I must have replied to the effect that it was not a question of art but of common reason, and that the artist's province did not extend to making bricks without straw or making two and two into five; and the work fell through. But had I the same thing to deal with now I should waste no words on it, but run the "ladder" right up out of the panel into the grisaille above; an opportunity for one of those delightful naïve *exceptions* of which old art is so full—like, for instance, the west door of St. Maclou at Rouen, where the crowd of falling angels burst out of the tympanum, bang through the lintel, defying architecture as they defied the first great Architect, and continue their fall amongst the columns below. "Angels Descending," by-the-bye, with a vengeance! And if the bad ones, why not the good? I might just as well have done it, and probably it would have been the very thing out of the whole commission which would have prevented the series from being the tame things that such sometimes are. Anyway, remember this—for I have invariably found it true—that *the chief difficulty of a work of art is always its chief opportunity.* A thing can be looked at in a thousand and one ways, and something dauntingly impossible will often be the very thing that will shake your jogtrot cart out of its rut, make you whip up your horses, and get you right home.

BUT

Observe this—that all these wishes of the client should be most strictly ascertained *beforehand*; all possibility of midway criticism and alteration prevented. Thresh the thing well out in the preliminary stages and start clear; as long as it *is* raw material, all in solution, all hanging in the balance—you can do anything. It is like "clay in the hands of the potter," and you can make the vessel as you please: "Out of the same lump making one vessel to honour and another to dishonour." But when the work is *half-done*, when colour is calling out to colour, and shape to shape, and thought to thought, throughout the length and breadth of the work;

when the ideas and the clothing of them are all fusing together into one harmony; when, in short, the thing is becoming that indestructible, unalterable unity which we call a Work of Art:—then, indeed, to be required to change or to reconsider is a real agony of impossibility; tearing the glowing web of thought, and form, and fancy into a destruction never to be reconstructed, and which no piecing or patching will mend.

There are many minor points, but they are really so entirely matters of experience, that it hardly seems worth while to dwell upon them. Start with recognising the fact that you must try to add business habits and sensible and economical ways to your genius as an artist; in short, another whole side to your character; and keep that ever in view, and the details will fall into their places.

Have Everything in Order.—Every letter relating to a current job should be findable at a moment's notice in an office "letter basket," rather wider than a sheet of foolscap paper, and with sides high enough to allow of the papers standing upright in unfolded sheets, each group of them behind a card taller than the tallest kind of ordinary document, and bearing along the top edge in large red letters—Roman capitals for choice—the name of the work: and it need hardly be said that these should be arranged in alphabetical order. For minor matters too small for such classification it is well to have, in the *front* place in the basket, cards dividing the alphabet itself into about four parts, so that unarranged small matters can be still kept roughly alphabetical. When the work is done, transfer all documents to separate labelled portfolios—a folded sheet of the thickest brown paper, such as they put under carpets, is very good—and store them away for reference. Larger portfolios for all *templates*, tracings, or architects' details or drawings relating to the work. If you have not a good system with regard to the ordering of these things, believe me the mere *administration* of a very moderate amount of work will take you *all your day*.

So also with *measurement*.

ON ACCURACY IN MEASUREMENT.

In one of Turgenieff's novels a Russian country proverb is quoted—"Measure thrice, cut once." It is a golden rule, and should be inscribed in the heart of every worker, and I will add one that springs out of it—"Never trust a measurement unless it has been made by yourself, or for yourself—to your order."

The measurements on architects' designs, or even working drawings, can never be trusted for the dimensions of the built work. Even the builders' templates, by which the work was built, cannot be, for the masons knock these quite enough out, in actual building, to make your work done by these guides a misfit. Have your own measurements taken again. Above all, beware of trusting to the supposed verticals or horizontals in built work, especially in tracery. A thing may be theoretically and intentionally at a certain angle, but actually at quite a different one. If level is important, take it yourself with spirit-level and plumb-line.

With regard to accuracy of work *in the shop*, where it depends on yourself and the system you observe, I cannot do better than write out for you here the written notice by which the matter is regulated in my own practice with regard to cartoons.

"Rules to be Observed in Setting out Forms for Cartoons.

"In every case of setting out any form, or batch of forms, for new windows the truth of the first long line ruled must be *tested* by stretching a thread.

If the lath is proved to be out, it must at once be sent to a joiner to be accurately 'shot,' and the accuracy of *both* its edges must then be tested with a thread.

The first right angle made (for the corner of the form) must also be tested by raising a perpendicular, with a radius of the compasses not less than 6 inches and with a needle-pointed pencil, and by the subjoined formula and no other.

From a given point in a given straight line to raise a perpendicular. Let A B be the given straight line (this must be the *long* side of the form, and the point B must be one corner of the base-line): it is required to raise from the point B a line perpendicular to the line A B.

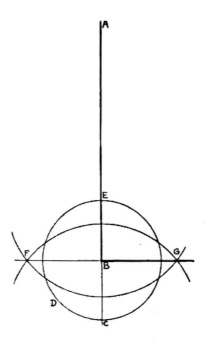

FIG. 71.

(1) Prolong the line A B at least 6 inches beyond B (if there is not room on the paper, it must be pinned on to a smooth board, and a piece of paper pinned on, so as to meet the edge of it, and continue it to the required distance).

(2) With the centre B (the compass leg being in all cases placed with absolute accuracy, using a lens if necessary to place it) describe the circle C D E.

(3) With the centres C and E, and with a radius of not less than 9 inches, describe arcs intersecting at F and G.

(4) Join F G.

Then, if the work has been correctly done, the line F G will *pass through the point* B, and be perpendicular to the line A B. If it does not do so, the work is incorrect, and must be repeated.

When the base and the springing-line are drawn on the form, the form must be accurately measured from the bottom upwards, and *every foot marked on both sides*. Such markings to be in fine pencil-line, and to be drawn from the sides of the form to the extreme margin of the paper, and you are not to trust your eye by laying the lath flat down and ticking off opposite the inch-marks, but you are to stand the lath on its edge, so that the inch-marks actually meet the paper, and then tick opposite to them.

Also if there are any bars in the window to be observed, the places of these must be marked, and it must be made quite clear whether the mark is the middle of the bar or its edge; and all this marking must be done lightly, but very carefully, with a needle-pointed pencil.

In every case where the forms are set out from templates, the accuracy of the templates must be verified, and in the event of the base not being at right angles with the side, a true horizontal must be made from the corner which is higher than the other (the one therefore which has the obtuse angle) and marked within the untrue line; and all measurements, whether of feet, bars, or squaring-out lines, or levels for canopies, bases, or any other divisions of the light, must be made upwards FROM THIS TRUE LEVEL LINE."

These rules, I suppose, have saved me on an average an hour a day since they were drawn up; and, mark you, an hour of *waste* and an hour of *worry* a day—which is as good as saving a day's work at the least.

An artist must dream; you will not charge me with undervaluing that; but a decorator must also wake, and have his wits about him! Start, therefore, in all the outward ordering of your career with the three plain rules:—

(1) To have everything orderly;

(2) To have everything accurate;

(3) To bring everything and every question to a point, *at the time*, and clinch it.

CHAPTER XX

A STRING OF BEADS

Is there anything more to say?

A whole world-full, of course; for every single thing is a part of all things. But I have said most of my say; and I could now wish that you were here that you might ask me aught else you want.

A few threads remain that might be gathered up—parting words, hints that cannot be classified. I must string them together like a row of beads; big and little mixed; we will try to get the big ones more or less in the middle if we can.

Grow everything from seed.

All seeds that are living (and therefore worth growing) have the power in them to grow.

But so many people miss the fact that, on the other hand, *nothing else* will grow; and that it is useless in art to transplant full-grown trees.

This is the key to great and little miseries, great and little mistakes.

Were you sorry to be on the lowest step of the ladder? Be glad; for all your hopes of climbing are in that.

And this applies in all things, from conditions of success and methods of "getting work" up to the highest questions of art and the "steps to Parnassus," by which are reached the very loftiest of ideals.

I must not linger over the former of these two things or do more than sum it up in the advice, to take anything you can get, and to be glad, not sorry, if it is small and comes to you but slowly. Simple things, and little things, and many things, are more needed in the arts today than complex things and great and isolated achievements. If you have nothing to do for others, do some little thing for yourself: it is a seed, presently it will send out a shoot of your first "commission," and that will probably lead to two others, or to a larger one; but pray to be led by small steps; and make sure of firm footing as you go, for there is such a thing as trying to take a *leap* on the ladder, and leaping off it.

So much for the seed of success.

The seed of craftsmanship I have tried to describe in this book.

The seed of ornament and design, it is impossible to treat of here; it would require as large a book as this to itself: but I will hazard the devotion of a page each to the A and the B of my own A B C of the subject as I try to teach it to my pupils, and put them before you without comment, hoping they may be of some slight use. (See figs. 72 and 73.)

But though I said that nothing will grow but seed, it does not, of course, follow that every seed will grow, or, if it does, that you yourself will reap the exact harvest you expect, or even recognise it in its fruitage as the growth of what you have sown. Expect to give much for little, to lose sight of the bread cast on the waters, not even sure that you will know it again even if you find it after many days. You never know, and therefore do not count your scalps too carefully or try to number your Israel and Judah. Neither, on the other hand, allow your seed to be forced by the hothouse of advertising or business pushing, or anything which will distract or distort that quiet gaze upon the work by which you love it for its own sake, and judge it on its merits; all such sidelights are misleading, since you do not know whether it is intended that this or that shall prosper or both be alike good.

How many a man one sees, earnest and sincere at starting, led aside off the track by the false lights of publicity and a first success. Art is peace. Do things because you love them. If purple is your favourite colour, put purple in your window; if green, green; if yellow, yellow. Flowers and leaves and buds because you love them. Glass because you love it. It is not that you are to despise either fame or wealth. Honestly acquired both are good. But you must bear in mind that the pursuit of these separately by any other means than perfecting your work is a thing requiring great outlay of TIME, and you cannot afford to withdraw any time from your work in order to acquire them.

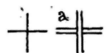

FIG. 72: Design consists of arrangement. Let us practise arrangement separately, and on its simplest terms. Take the simplest possible arranged form, and make all ornament spring from this, without, for a considerable time changing its character, or making any additions of a different character to it. If we are not then to do this what resource have we? we may change its direction. Proceed then to do so, observing a few very simple rules.

1. Do the work in single "stitches" 2. & to each arm of the cross in turn. 3 keep a record of each step; that is, as soon as you have got any definite development from your original form, put that down on paper and leave it, drawing it over again and developing from the second drawing.

The fourth rule is the most important of all: 4. Keep "on the spot" as much as possible, i.e. take a number of single steps from the point you have arrived at, not a number of consecutive steps leading farther from it.

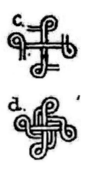

For example: "b" here is a single step from "a", you do one thing. I do not want you to go on developing from it [fig. "b"] as "c", "d" & "e" until you have gone back to fig. "a" and made all the immediately possible steps to be taken from it, one of which is shown, fig "f."

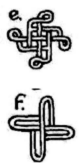

FIG. 73: Seed of design as applied to Craft & Material.

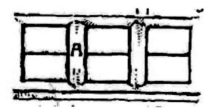

Suppose you have three simple openings. (fig. 'a'.) garret windows, or passage windows, we will suppose, each with a central horizontal bar: and suppose you have a number of pieces of glass to use up already cut to one gauge, and that

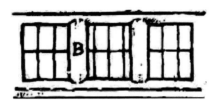

six of these fill a window, can you get any little variety by arrangement on the following terms. 1. Treating both upper and lower ranges alike 2. Allowing yourself to halve them, vertically only. 3. Not wasting any glass.

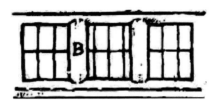

4. Not halving more than two in each light. How is this, fig. b? you despise it? so absurdly simple? It is the key to all simple ornament in leaded glass. Exhaust all the possible varieties, there are at least nine. Do them. That's all.

In these days and in our huge cities there are so many avenues open to celebrity, through Society, the Press, Exhibition, and so forth, that a man once led to spend time on them is in danger of finding half his working life run away with by them before he is aware, while even if they are successful the success won by them is a poor thing compared to that which might have been earned by the work which was sacrificed for them. It becomes almost a profession in itself to keep oneself notorious.

To spend large slices out of one's time in the mere putting forward of one's work, *showing* it apart from *doing* it, necessary as this sometimes is, is a thing to be done grudgingly; still more so should one grudge to be called from one's work here, there, and everywhere by the social claims which crowd round the position of a public man.

There are strenuous things enough for you in the work itself without wasting your strength on these. We will speak of them presently; but a word first upon originality.

Don't *strive* to be original; no one ever got Heaven's gift of invention by saying, "I must have it, and since I don't feel it I must assume it and pretend it;" follow rather your master patiently and lovingly for a long time; give and take, echo his habits as Botticelli echoed Filippo Lippi's, but improve upon them; add something to them if you can, as he also did, and pass then on, as he also did, to the *little* Filippo—Filippino—making him a truer and sweeter heart than his father, out of the well of truth and sweetness with which Botticelli's own heart was brimming. Do this, but at the same time expect with happy patience, as a boy longs for his manhood, yet does not try to hasten it and does not pretend to forestall it, the time when some fresh idea in imagination, some fresh method in design, some fresh process in craftsmanship, will come to you as a reward of patient working—and come by accident, as all such things do, lest you should think it your own and miss the joy of knowing that it is not yours but Heaven's.

And when this comes, guard it and mature it carefully. Do not throw it out too lavishly broadcast with the ostentation of a generous genius having gifts to spare. Share it with proved and worthy friends, when they notice it and ask you about it, but in the meanwhile develop and cultivate it as a gardener does a tree. And this leads me to the most important point of all—namely, the value, the all-sufficing value, of *one* new step on the road of Beauty. If such is really granted you, consider it as enough for your lifetime. One such thing in the history of the arts has generally been enough for a century; how much more, then, for a generation.

For indeed there is only one rule for fine work in art, that you should put your whole strength, all the powers of mind and body into every touch. Nothing less will do than that. You must face it in drawing from the life. Try it in its acutest form, not from the posed, professional model, who will sit like a stone; try it with children, two years old or so; the despair of it, the exhaustion: and then, in a flash, when you thought you had really done somewhat, a still more captivating, fascinating gesture, which makes all you have done look like lead. Can you screw your exhaustion up *again*, sacrifice all you have done, and face the labour of wrestling with the new idea? And if you do? You are sick with doubt between the new and the old. You ask your friends; you probably choose wrong; your judgment is clouded by the fatigue of your previous toil.

But you have gained strength. That is the real point of the thing. It is not what you have done in this instance, but what you have become in doing it. Next time, fresh and strong, you will dash the beautiful sudden thought upon the paper and leave it, happy to make others happy, but only through the pains you took before, which are a small price to pay for the joy of the strength you have gained.

This is the rule of great work. Puzzle and hesitation and compromise can only occur because you have left some factor of the problem out of count, and this should never be. Your business is to take all into account and to sacrifice everything, however fascinating and tempting it may be in itself, if it does not fit in as part of an harmonious *whole*. Remember in this case, when loth to make such sacrifice, the old saying that "there's as good fish in the sea as ever came out." Brace yourself to try for something still better. Recast your composition. If it is defective, the defect all comes from some want of strenuousness as you went along. It is like getting a bit of your figure out of drawing because your eye only measured some portion of it with one or two portions of the rest and not with the whole figure and attitude. Every student knows the feeling. So in your composition: you may get impossible levels, impossible relations between the subject and the surrounding canopy: perhaps one coming in front of the other at one point and the reverse at another point. You drew the thing dreamily: you were not alert enough. And now you must waste what you had got to love, because though it's so pretty it is not fitting.

But sometimes it will happen that some line of your composition is thus hacked off by no fault of yours, by some mismeasurement of a bar by your builder, or some change of mind or whim of your client, who "likes it all but"——(some vital feature). As we have said, this is not quite a fair demand to be made upon the artist, but it will sometimes occur, whatever we do. Pull yourself together, and, before you stand out about it and refuse to change, consider. Try the modification, and try it in such an aroused and angry spirit as shall flame out against the difficulty with force and heat. Let the whole thing be as fuel of fire, and the reward will be given. The chief difficulty may become—it is more than an even chance that it does become—the chief glory, and that the composition will be like the new-born Ph[œ]nix, sprung from the ashes of the old and thrice as fair.

Then also strike while the iron is hot, and work while you're warm to it. When you have done the main figure-study and slain its difficulty you feel braced up, your mind clear, and you see your way to link it in with the surroundings. Will you let it all get cold because it is toward evening and you are physically tired, when another hour would set the whole problem right for next day's work; now, while you are warm, while the beauty of the model you have drawn from is still glowing in you with a thousand suggestions and possibilities? You will do in another hour now what would take you days to do when the fire has died down—if you ever do it at all.

It is after a day's work such as this that one feels the true delight of the balm of Nature. For conquered difficulty brings new insight through the feeling of new power; and new beauties are seen because they are felt to be attainable, and by virtue of the assurance that one has got distinctly a step nearer to the veil that hides the inner heart of things which is our destined home.

It is after work like this, feeling the stirrings of some real strength within you, promising power to deal with nature's secrets by-and-by, that you see as never before the beauty of things.

The keen eyes that have been so busy turn gratefully to the silver of the sky with the grey, quiet trees against it and the watery gleam of sunset like pale gold, low down behind the boughs, where the robin, half seen, is flitting from place to place, choosing his rest and twittering his good-night; and you think with good hope of your life that is coming, and of all your aspirations and your dreams. And in the stillness and the coolness and the peace you can dwell with confidence upon the thought of all the Unknown that is moving onward towards you, as the glow which is fading renews itself day by day in the East, bringing the daily task with it.

You feel that you are able to meet it, and that all is well; that there are quiet and good things in store, and that this constant renewal of the glories of day and night, this constant procession of morning and evening as the world rolls round, has become almost a special possession to you, to which only those who pay the price have entrance, an inheritance of your own as a reward of your endeavour and acquired power, and leading to some purposed end that will be peace.

Stained-glass, stained-glass, stained-glass! At night in the lofty church windows the bits glow and gloom and talk to one another in their places; and the pictured angels and saints look down, peopling the empty aisles and companioning the lamp of the sanctuary.

The beads worth threading seem about all threaded now, and the book appears to be done. Thus we have gone on then, making it as it came to hand, blundering, as it seems to me, on the borders of half a dozen literary or illiterate styles, the pen not being the tool of our proper craft; but on the whole saying somehow what we meant to say: laughing when we felt amused, and being serious when the subject seemed so, our object being indeed to make workers in stained-glass and not a book about it. Is it worth while to try and put a little clasp to our string of beads and tie all together?

There was a little boy (was he six or seven or eight?), and his seat on Sunday was opposite the door in the fourteenth-century chancel of the little Norman country church. There the great, tall windows hung in the air around him, and he used to stare up at them with goggle-eyes in the way that used to earn him household names, wondering which he liked best. And for months one would be the favourite, and for months another would supplant it; his fancy would change, and now he liked this—now that. Only the stone tracery-bars, for there was no stained-glass to spoil them. The broad, plain flagstones of the floor spread round him in cool, white spaces, in loved unevenness, honoured by the foot-tracks which had worn the stone into little valleys from the door and through the narrow, Norman chancel-arch up towards the altar rails, telling of generations of feet, long since at rest, that had carried simple lives to seek the place as the place of their help or peace.

Plain rush-plaited hassocks and little brass sconces where, on lenten nights, in the unwarmed church, glimmered the few candles that lit the devotion of the strong, rough sons of the glebe, hedgers and ditchers, who came there after daily labour to spell out simple prayer and praise. But it was best on the summer Sunday mornings, when the great spaces of blue, and the towering white clouds looked down through the diamond panes; and the iron-studded door, with the wonderful big key, which his hands were not yet strong enough to turn, stood wide open; and outside, amongst the deep grass that grew upon the graves, he could see the tortoise-shell butterflies sunning themselves upon the dandelions. Then it was that he used to think the outside the best, and fancy (with perfect truth, as I believe) that angels must be looking in, just as much as he was looking out, and gazing down, grave-eyed, upon the little people inside, as he himself used to watch the red ants busy in their tiny mounds upon the grass plot or the gravel path; and he wondered sometimes whether the outside or the inside was "God's House" most: the place where he was sitting, with rough, simple things about him that the village carpenter or mason or blacksmith had made, or the beautiful glowing world outside. And as he thought, with the grave mind of a child, about these things, he came to fancy that the eyes that looked out through the silver diamond-panes which kept out the wind and rain, mattered less than the eyes that looked in from the other side where basked the butterflies and flowers and all the living things he so loved; awful eyes that were at home where hung the sun himself in his distances and the stars in the great star-spaces; where Orion and the Pleiades glittered in the winter nights, where "Mazzaroth was brought forth in his season," and where through the purple skies of summer evening was laid out overhead the assigned path along which moved Arcturus with his sons.

APPENDIX I

SOME SUGGESTIONS AS TO THE STUDY OF OLD GLASS

Every one who wants to study glass should go to York Minster. Go to the extreme west end, the first two windows are of plain quarries most prettily leaded, and showing how pleasant "plain-glazing" may be, with silvery glass and a child-like enjoyment of simple patterning, unconscious of "high art." But look at the second window on the north side. What do you see? You see a yellow shield? Exactly. Every one who looks at that window as he passes at a quick walk must come away remembering that he had seen a yellow shield. But stop and look at it. Don't you *like* it—*I* do! Why?—well, because it happens to be by good luck just *right*, and it is a very good lesson of the degree in which beauty in glass depends on juxtaposition. I had thought of it as a particularly beautiful bit of glass in quality and colour—but not at all! it is textureless and rather crude. I had thought of it as old—not at all: it is probably eighteenth-century. But look what it happens to be set in—the mixture of agate, silver, greenish and black quarries. Imagine it by itself without the dull citron crocketting and pale yellow-stain "sun" and "shafting" of the panel below—without the black and yellow escutcheon in the light to its right hand—even without the cutting up and breaking with black lead lines of its own upper half. In short, you could have it so placed that you would like it no better, that it would *be* no better, than the bit of "builder's glazing" in the top quatrefoil of the next window, which looks like, and I fancy is, of almost the very same glass, but clumsily mixed, and, fortunately, *dated* for our instruction, 1779.

I do not know any place where you can get more study of certain properties of glass than in the city of York. The cathedral alone is a mine of wealth. The nave windows are near enough to see all necessary detail. There is something of every period. And with regard to the nave and clerestory windows, they have been so mauled and re-leaded that you need not be in the least afraid of admiring the wrong thing or passing by the right. You can be quite frank and simple about it all. For instance, my own favourite window is the fifth from the west on the south side. The old restorer has coolly slipped down one whole panel below its proper level in a shower of rose-leaves (which were really, I believe, originally a pavement), and, frankly, I don't know (and don't care) whether they are part of his work in the late eighteenth century or the original glass of the late fourteenth. I rather incline to think that they came out of some other window and are bits of fifteenth-century glass. The same with the chequered shield of Vernon in the other light. I daresay it is a bit of builder's glazing—but isn't it jolly? And what do you think of the colour of the little central circle half-way up the middle light? Isn't it a flower? And look at the petal that's dropped from it on to the bar below! or the *whole* of the left-hand light; well, or the middle light, or the right-hand light? If that's not colour I don't know what is. I doubt if it was any more beautiful when it was new, perhaps not so beautiful. Compare it, for example, with the window in the same wall (I think next to it on the west, which has been "restored"). The window exactly opposite seems one of the least retouched, and the least interesting; if you think the yellow canopies disagreeable in colour don't be ashamed to say so: they are not unbeautiful exactly, I think, but, personally, I could do with less of them. Yet I should not be surprised to be assured that they are all genuine fourteenth-century. In the north transept is the celebrated "Five Sisters," the most beautiful bit of thirteenth-century "grisaille" perhaps in existence. That is where we get our patterns for "kamptulicon" from; but we don't make kamptulicon quite like it. If you want a sample of "nineteenth-century thirteenth-century" work you have only to look over your left shoulder.

A similar glance to the right will show you "nineteenth-century fifteenth-century" work—and show it you in a curious and instructive transition stage— portions of the two right-hand windows of the five being old glass worked in with new, while the right-hand one of all is a little abbot who is nearly all old and has shrunk behind a tomb, wondering, as it seems to me, "how those fellows got in," and making up his mind whether he's going to stand being bullied by the new St. Peter. In the south transept opposite, all the five eastern windows are fifteenth-century, and some of them very well preserved, while those in the southern wall are modern. The great east window has a history of its own quite easily ascertainable on the spot and worthy of research and study. Then go into the north ambulatory, look at the third of the big windows. Well, the right-hand light; look at the bishop at the top in a dark red chasuble, note the bits of dull rose colour in the lower dress, the bit of blackish grey touching the pastoral staff just below the edge of the chasuble, look at the bits of sharp strong blue in the background. Now I believe these are all accidents—bits put in in releading; but when the choir is singing and you can pick out every separate note of the harmony as it comes down to you from each curve of the fretted roof, if you don't think this window goes with it and is music also, you must be wrong, I think, in eye or ear. But indeed this part of the church and all round the choir aisles on both sides is a perfect treasure-house of glass.

If you want an instance of what I said (p. 212) as to "added notes turning discord into harmony," look at the *patched* east window of the south choir aisle. Mere jumble—probably no selection—yet how beautiful! like beds of flowers. Did you ever see a bed of flowers that was *not* beautiful?—often and often, when the gardener had carefully selected the plants of his ribbon-bordering; but I would have you think of an old-fashioned cottage garden, with its roses and lilies and larkspur and snapdragon and marigolds—those are what windows should be like.

In addition to the minster, almost every church in the city has some interesting glass; several of them a great quantity, and some finer than any in the cathedral itself. And here I would give a hint. *Never pass a church or chapel of any sort or kind, old or new, without looking in.* You cannot tell what you may find.

And a second hint. Do not make written pencil notes regarding colour, either from glass or nature, for you'll never trouble to puzzle them out afterwards. Take your colour-box with you. The merest dot of tint on the paper will bring everything back to mind.

Space prevents our making here anything like a complete itinerary setting forth where glass may be studied; it must suffice to name a few centres, noting a few places in the same district which may be visited from them easily. I name only those I know myself, and of course the list is very slight.

YORK. And all churches in the city.

GLOUCESTER. Tewkesbury, Cirencester.

BIRMINGHAM. (For Burne-Jones glass.) Shrewsbury, Warwick, Tamworth, Malvern.

WELLS.

OXFORD. Much glass in the city, old and new. Fairford.

CAMBRIDGE. Much glass in the city, old and new.

CANTERBURY.

CHARTRES. (If there is still any left unrestored.) St. Pierre in the same town.

SENS.

TROYES. AUXERRE.

Of the last two I have only seen some copies. For glass by Rossetti, Burne-Jones, and Madox-Brown, consult their lives.

There are many well-known books on the subject of ancient glass, Winston, Westlake, &c., which give fuller details on this matter.

APPENDIX II

ON THE RESTORING OF ANCIENT WINDOWS

Let us realise what *is* done.

And let us consider what *ought to be done.*

A window of ancient glass needs releading. The lead has decayed and the whole is loose and shaky. The ancient glass has worn very thin, pitted almost through like a worn-out thimble with little holes where the alkalis have worked their way out. It is as fragile and tender as an old oil-painting that needs to be taken off a rotten canvas and re-lined. If you examine a piece of old glass whose lead has had time to decay, you will find that the glass itself is often in an equally tender state. The painting would remain for years, probably for centuries yet, if untouched, just as dust, without any attachment at all, will hang on a vertical looking-glass. But if you scrape it, even only with the finger-nail, you will generally find that that is sufficient to bring much—perhaps most—of the painting off, while both sides of the glass are covered with a "patina" of age which is its chief glory in quality and colour, and which, or most of which, a wet handkerchief dipped in a little dust and rubbed smartly will remove.

In short, here is a work of art as beautiful and precious as a picture by Titian or Holbein, and probably, as being the chief glory of some stately cathedral, still more precious, which ought only to be trusted to the gentle hands of a cultivated and scientific artist, connoisseur, and expert. The glass should all be handled as if it were old filigree silver. If the lead is so perished that it is absolutely impossible to avoid taking the glass down, it should be received on the scaffold itself, straight from its place in the stone, between packing-boards lined with sheets of wadding—"cotton-wool"—attached to the boards with size or paste, and with, of course, the "fluffy" side outwards. These boards, section by section, should be finally corded or clamped ready for travelling *before being lowered from the scaffold*; if any pieces of the glass get detached they should be carefully packed in separate boxes, each labelled with a letter corresponding to one placed on the section as packed, so that there may be no chance of their place ever being lost, and when all is done the whole window will be ready to be gently lowered, securely "packed for removal," to the pavement below. The ideal thing now would be to hire a room and do the work on the spot; but if this is impossible on account of expense and the thing has to bear a journey, the sections, packed as above described, should be themselves packed, two or three together, as may be convenient, in an outer packing-case for travelling. It should be insured, for then a representative of the railway must attend to certify the packing, and also extra care will be taken in transit.

Arrived at the shop, the window should be laid out carefully on the bench and each bit re-leaded into its place, the very fragile pieces between two bits of thin sheet-glass.

Unless this last practice is adopted *throughout*, the ordinary process of cementing must be omitted and careful puttying substituted for it. While if it *is* adopted the whole must be puttied *before* cementing, otherwise the cement will run in between the various thicknesses of glass. It would be an expensive and tedious and rather thankless process, for the repairer's whole aim would be to hide from the spectator the fact that anything whatever had been done.

What does happen at present is this. A country clergyman, or, in the case of a cathedral, an architectural surveyor, neither of whom know by actual practice anything technically of stained-glass, hand the job over to some one representing a stained-glass establishment. This gentleman has studied stained-glass on paper, and knows as much about cutting or leading technically and by personal practice, as an architect does of masonry, or stone-carving—neither more nor less. That is to say, he has made sketch-books full of water-colour or pencil studies, and endless notes from old examples, and has never cut a bit of glass in his life, or leaded it.

Well, he assumes the responsibility, and the client reposes in the blissful confidence that all is well.

Is all well?

The work is placed in the charge of the manager, and through him it filters down as part of the ordinary, natural course of events into the glazing-shop. Here this precious and fragile work of art we have described is handed over to a number of ordinary working men to treat by the ordinary methods of their trade. They know perfectly well that nobody above them knows as much as they, or, indeed, anything at all of their craft. Division of labour has made them "glaziers," as it has made the gentlemen above stairs, who do the cartoons or the painting, "artists." These last know nothing of glazing, why should glaziers know anything of art? It is perfectly just reasoning; they do their very best, and what they do is this. They take out the old, tender glass, with the colour hardly clinging to it, and they put it into fresh leads, and then they solder up the joints. And, by way of a triumphant wind-up to a good, solid, English, common-sense job, with no art-nonsense or fads about it, they proceed to scrub the whole on both sides with stiff grass-brushes (ordinarily sold at the oil-shops for keeping back-kitchen sinks clean), using with them a composition mainly consisting of exactly the same materials with which a housemaid polishes the fender and fire-irons. That is a plain, simple, unvarnished statement of facts. You may find it difficult of belief, but this is what actually happens. This is what you are having done everywhere, guardians of our ancient buildings. You'll soon have all your old windows "quite as good as new." It's a merry world, isn't it?

APPENDIX III

Hints for the Curriculum of a Technical School for Stained-Glass—
Examples for Painting—Examples of Drapery—Drawing from Nature—
Ornamental Design.

Examples for Painting.—I have already recommended for outline work the splendid reproductions of the Garter Plates at Windsor. It is more difficult to find equally good examples for *painting*; for if one had what one wished it would be photographed from ideal painted-glass or else from cartoons wisely prepared for glass-work. But, in the first case, if the photographs were from the best ancient glass—even supposing one could get them—they would be unsatisfactory for two reasons. First, because ancient glass, however well preserved, has lost or gained something by age which no skill can reproduce; and secondly, because however beautiful it is, all but the very latest (and therefore not the best) is immature in drawing. It is not wise to reproduce those errors. The things themselves look beautiful and sincere because the old worker drew as well as he could; but if we, to imitate them, draw less well than we can, we are imitating the *accidents* of his production, and not the *method* and *principle* of it: the principle was to draw as well as he could, and we, if we wish to emulate old glass, must draw as well as *we* can. For examples of Heads nothing can be better than photographs from Botticelli and other early Tuscan, and from the early Siennese painters. Also from Holbein, and chiefly from his drawings. There is a flatness and firmness of treatment in all these which is eminently suited to stained-glass work. Hands also may be studied from the same sources, for though Botticelli does not always draw hands with perfect mastery, yet he very often does, and the expression of them, as of his heads, is always dignified and full of sweetness and gentleness of feeling; and as soon as we have learnt our craft so as to copy these properly, the best thing is to draw hands and heads for ourselves.

Examples of Drapery.—To me there is no drapery so beautiful and appropriate for stained-glass work in the whole world of art, ancient or modern, as that of Burne-Jones, and especially in his studies and drawings and cartoons for glass; and if these are not accessible, at least we may pose drapery as like it as we can, and draw it ourselves and copy it. But I would, at any rate, earnestly warn the student against the "crinkly-crankly" drapery imitated from Dürer and his school, which fills up the whole panel with wrinkles and "turnovers" (the linings of a robe which give an opportunity for changing the colour), and spreads out right and left and up and down till the poor bishop himself (and in nine cases out of ten it *is* a bishop, so that he may be mitred and crosiered and pearl-bordered) becomes a mere peg to hang vestments on, and is made short and dumpy for that end.

There is a great temptation and a great danger here. This kind of work, where every inch of space is filled with ornament and glitter, and change and variety and richness, is indeed in many ways right and good for stained-glass; which is a broken-up thing; where large blank spaces are to be avoided, and where each little bit of glass should look "cared for" and thought of, as a piece of fine jewellery is put together in its setting; and if craftsmanship were everything, much might be said for these methods. There is indeed plenty of stained-glass of the kind more beautiful as *craftsmanship* than anything since the Middle Ages, much more beautiful and cunning in workmanship than Burne-Jones, and yet which is little else but vestments and curtains and diaper—where there is no lesson taught, no subject dwelt on, no character studied or portrayed. If we wish it to be so—if we have nothing to teach or learn, if we wish to be let alone, to be soothed and lulled by mere sacred *trappings*, by pleasant colours and fine and delicate sheen and the glitter of silk and jewels—well and good, these things will serve; but if they fail to satisfy, go to St. Philip's, Birmingham, and see the solemnities and tragedies of Life and Death and Judgment, and all this will dwindle down into the mere upholstery and millinery that it is.

Drawing from Nature.—There is a side of drawing practice almost wholly neglected in schools, which consists, not in training the eye and hand to correctly measure and outline spaces and forms, but in training the finger-ends with an H.B. pencil point at the end of them to illustrate texture and minute detail. It is necessary to look at things in a large way, but it is equally necessary to look at them in a small way; to be able to count the ribs on a blade of grass or a tiny cockle-shell, and to give them in pencil, each with its own light and shade. I find the whole key to this teaching to lie in one golden rule—*not to frighten or daunt the student with big tasks at first.* A single grain of wheat, not a whole ear of corn; some tiny seed, tiny shell; but whatever *is* chosen, to be pursued with a needle-pointed pencil to the very verge of lens-work. I must yet again quote Ruskin. "You have noticed," he says, "that all great sculptors, and most of the great painters of Florence, began by being goldsmiths. Why do you think the goldsmith's apprenticeship is so fruitful? Primarily, because it forces the boy to do small work and mind what he is about. Do you suppose Michael Angelo learned his business by dashing or hitting at it?"

Ornamental Design.—It is impossible here to enter into a description of any system of teaching ornament. At p. 294 I have given just as much as two pages can give of the seed from which such a thing may spring. In some of the collotypes from the finished glass the patterns on quarry or robe which spring from this seed may be traced—very imperfectly, but as well as the scale and the difficulties of photography and the absence of colour will allow.

What I find best, in commencing with any student, is to start four practices together, and keep them going together step by step, side by side, through the course, one evening for each, or some like division.

Technical Work.—Cutting, glazing, &c.

Painting Work.—By graduated examples, from simple outline up to a head of Botticelli.

Ornament, as described; and

Drawing from Nature, in the spirit and methods we have spoken of.

Moulding the whole into a system of composition and execution, tempered and governed as it goes along by judiciously chosen reading and reference to examples, ancient or modern.

NOTES ON THE COLLOTYPE PLATES

It is obvious that stained-glass cannot be adequately shown in book-illustration.

For instance, we cannot have either the scale of it or the colour—two rather vital exceptions. These collotypes are, therefore, put forth as mere diagrams for the use of students, to call their attention to certain definite points and questions of treatment, and no more pretending than if they were black-board drawings to give adequate pictures of what glass can be or should be.

This is one reason, too, for the omission of all attempt to reproduce ancient glass. It was felt that it should not be subjected to the indignity of such very imperfect representation, and especially as so many much larger books on the subject exist, where at least the *scale* is not so ill-treated.

But, besides, if one once began illustrating old glass, one would immediately seem to be setting standards for present-day guidance, and this could only be done (*if done*) with many annotations and exceptions and with a much larger range of examples than is possible here.

The following illustrations, therefore, show the attempts of a group of workers who have endeavoured to carry into practice the principles set forth in this book. It has not been found possible in all cases to get photographs from the actual glass—always a very difficult thing to do. The illustrations can be seen much better by the aid of a moderately strong reading-lens.

154

PLATE I.—*Part of East Window, St. Anselm's, Woodridings, Pinner, by Louis Davis.* The design, cartoons, and cut-line made, all the glass chosen and painted, and the leading superintended by the artist.

I.—Part of Window. St. Anselm's, Woodridings, Pinner.

PLATE II.—*Another portion of the same window, by the same. Scenes from the Life of St. Anselm.* Executed under the same conditions as the above. The freehand drawing and the varying thickness of the leads in the quarry work should be noted.

II.—Part of Window. St. Anselm's, Woodridings, Pinner.

156

PLATE III.—*Window in St. Peter's Church, Clapham Road—"Blessed are they that Mourn," by Reginald Hallward.* The *whole* of the work in this instance, including cutting, leading, &c., is done by the artist himself. As an instance of how little photography can do, it is worth while to describe such a small item as the *scroll* above the figure. This is of glass most carefully selected (or most skilfully treated with acid), so that the ground work varies from silvery-white to almost a pansy-purple, and on this the verse is illuminated in tones varying from pale primrose to the ruddiest gold—the whole forming a passage of lovely colour impossible to achieve by any system of "copying." It is work like this and the preceding that is referred to on p. 266.

III.—Window. St. Peter's Church, Clapham.

PLATE IV.—*Central part of Window in Cobham Church, Kent, by Reginald Hallward.* Executed under the same conditions as the preceding.

IV.—Part of Window. Cobham Church, Kent.

158

PLATE V.—*Part of Window in Ardrahan Church, Galway*—*"St. Robert" by Selwyn Image*. From the cartoon. See p. 83.

V.—Part of Window. Ardrahan, Galway.

PLATE VI.—*Two Designs for Domestic Glass, by Miss M. J. Newill.* From the
cartoons.

VI.—From Cartoons for Domestic Glass.

PLATE VII.—*"The Dream of St. Kenelm," by H. A. Payne.* The author had the pleasure of watching this work daily while in progress. It was done entirely by the artist's own hand, by way of a specimen "masterpiece" of craftsmanship, and the aim was to use to the full extent every resource of the material.

VII.—Window. "The Dream of St. Kenelm.

PLATE VIII.—*Six "Quarries"—"Day and Night," "The Spirit on the Face of the Waters," "Creation of Birds and Fishes," "Eden," and "The Parable of the Good Seed," by Pupils of H. A. Payne, Birmingham School of Art.* These lose very much by reduction, and should be seen with a lens magnifying 2-1/2 diameters. They are the designs of the pupils themselves (boys in their teens), and are examples of bold outline *untouched after tracing.* They are more elaborate than would be desirable for *ordinary* quarry glazing; being intended for interior work on a screen, to be seen close at hand with borrowed light.

VIII.—Quarries. (Size of originals, 4-1/2 by 4 ins.)

PLATE IX.—*Micro-photographs.* 1. *A piece of outline that has "fried" in the kiln.* Magnified 20 diameters. See p. 104.

2. *A small Diamond seen from above.* Magnified 10-1/2 diameters. The white horizontal line is the cutting edge.

3. *A larger Diamond that has been "reset."* That is to say, *re-ground:* the diagonal marks like a St. Andrew's Cross show the grinding down of the old facets by which the new cutting edge has been produced. Magnified 10-1/2 diameters.

4. No. 2 *seen from the side.* Magnified 10-1/2 diameters; the cutting edge faces towards the left.

IX.—Micro-photographs from details connected with Glass Work.

PLATE X.—*Micro-photographs of Glass-cutting* Very difficult to explain. "A" is a sheet of glass seen *in section* multiplied 15-1/2 diameters. The black marks along the *top edge* are diamond-cuts, good and bad, coming *straight towards the spectator.* The two outside ones are very *bad* cuts, far too violent, and have split off the surface of the glass. Of the two inner ones the left-hand one is an ideally good cut, no disturbance of the surface having occurred; the right-hand a fairly good one, but a little unnecessarily hard. Passing over B for the present—C is a similar piece of glass also magnified 15-1/2 diameters, with *wheel-cuts* seen endwise (coming towards the spectator). The one on the left is a very bad cut, the surface of the glass having actually split off in flakes, the next to it is a perfect cut where the surface is intact, and note that though not a quarter so much pressure has been employed, the split downward into the glass is deeper and sharper than in the violent cut to the left, as is also the case with the two other moderately good cuts to the right.

D, E—*Wheel-cuts.* In these we are looking down upon the surface of the glass. They are bad cuts, multiplied 20 diameters; the direction of the cut is from left to right. In the upper figure the flake of glass is split completely off but is still lying in its place. In the lower one the left-hand half is split, and the right-hand only partially so, remaining so closely attached to the body of the glass as to show (and in an especially beautiful and perfect manner) the rainbow-tinted "Newton's rings" which accompany the phenomenon of "Interference," for an explanation of which I must refer the reader to an encyclopædia or some work on optics. *Good* cuts seen from above are simply lines like a hair upon the glass, but the diamond-cut is a coarser hair than the wheel-cut.

If you now hold the illustration *upside down*, what then becomes the top edge of section C shows a wheel-cut seen sideways along the section of the glass which it has divided, the direction of this cut being from left to right.

In the same way section "A" seen upside down gives the appearance of a *diamond*-cut, also from left to right, and multiplied 15-1/2 diameters, while "B" held in the same position gives the same cut multiplied 78 diameters. The nature of these things is discussed at p. 48.

In their natural colour, and under strong light, they are very beautiful objects under the microscope. Even a 10-diameter "Steinheil lens," or still better its English equivalent, a Nelson lens, will show them fairly, and some such instrument, opening out a new world of beauty beyond the power of ordinary vision, ought, one would think, to be one of the possessions of every artist and lover of Nature.

The illustrations that follow are from the work of the author and his pupils conjointly. Those in which no *design* has been added are for clearness' sake described as "by the author"; but it is to be understood that in all instances the transcribing of the work *in the glass* has been the work of pupils under his supervision. All design of diaper, canopy, lettering, and quarries is so, in all the examples selected.

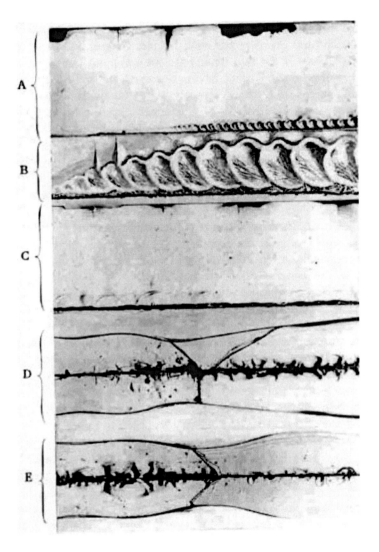

X.—Micro-photographs. Diamond and Wheel Cuts seen in Section and Plan.

PLATE XI.—*From Gloucester Cathedral*—*"St. Boniface" by the author and his pupils.*

XI.—Part of Window. Gloucester Cathedral.

PLATE XII.—*From the same*—*"The Stork of Iona" and "The Infant Church," by the same.* Canopies from Oak and Ivy.

XII.—Part of Window. Gloucester Cathedral.

PLATE XIII.—*Portion of a Window in progress (destined for Ashbourne Church), by the author.* This has been specially photographed *on the easel,* to show how near, by the use of false lead lines, &c., the work can be got, during its progress, to approach to its actual conditions when finished.

XIII.—Portion of Unfinished Window, photographed from Work on the Easel.

PLATE XIV.—*Drawings from Nature, by the author's pupils.* Pieced together from various drawings by three different hands; made in preparation for design of Oak "canopy." See p. 324 and Plate XI.

XIV.—Drawings from Nature, in Preparation for Design.

PLATE XV.—*Part of East Window of School Chapel, Tonbridge, by the author.*
From the cartoon: the figure playing the dulcimer is underneath the manger,
above which is seated the Virgin and Child.

**XV.—Part of Window. Tonbridge School Chapel, photographed from the
Cartoon.**

PLATE XVI.—*Figure of one of the Choir of "Dominations." From Gloucester, by the author and his pupils.*

XVI.—Part of Window. Gloucester Cathedral.

The names of the pupils whose work appears in Plate VIII. are J. H. Saunders and R. J. Stubington. In Plate XIV. A. E. Child, K. Parsons, and J. H. Stanley; and in the Plates XI. to XVI. J. Brett, L. Brett, A. E. Child, P. R. Edwards, M. Hutchinson, K. Parsons, J. H. Stanley, J. E. Tarbox, and E. A. Woore. The cuts in the text are by K. Parsons and E. A. Woore.

GLOSSARY

Antiques, coloured glasses made in imitation of the qualities of ancient glass.

Banding, putting on the copper "ties" by which the glazed light is attached to the supporting bars.

Base, (1) the light-tinted glass, white, greenish or yellow, on which the thin film of ruby or blue is imposed in "flashed" glasses; (2) the support of the niche on which the figure stands in "canopy work."

Borrowed light, a light not coming direct from daylight, but from the interior light of a building as in the case of a *screen* of glass. (The result is similar when a window is seen against near background of trees or buildings.)

Calm (of lead), the strip of lead, 3 to 4 feet long, as used for leading up the glass.

Canopy or "tabernacle work," the architectural framing in imitation of a carved niche in which the figure is placed. The vertical supports (sometimes used alone to frame in the whole light) are called "shafting."

Cartoon, the design of the window, full size, on paper.

Chasuble, the outermost sacrificial vestment of a bishop or priest.

Cope, the outermost ceremonial and processional vestment of a bishop or priest.

Core (of lead), the crossbar of the "H" section as shown in fig. 34.

Crocketting, the ornamenting of any architectural member at intervals with sculptured bosses or crockets.

Cullet, the waste cuttings of glass. Generally used over again in greater or less quantity as an ingredient in the making of new glass.

Cut-line, the tracing (containing the lead lines only) by which the work is cut and glazed.

Flux, the solvent which assists the melting of the metallic pigments in the kiln. Various materials are used, *e.g.* silica and lead, but unfortunately borax also is used, and I would warn the student to buy no pigment without a guarantee from the manufacturer that it does not contain this tempting but very dangerous and unstable ingredient. (See p. 112).

Form, the sheet of "continuous cartridge" or cartoon paper on which the dimensions, &c., are marked out for drawing the cartoon.

Gauge, (1) the shaped piece of paper by which the diamond is guided in cutting; (2) the standard of size and shape in any piece of repeated work (as quarry-glazing).

Grisaille (from Fr. *gris*, grey), work where a pattern, generally geometrical, in narrow coloured bands, is superimposed on a background of whitish, grey, or greenish glass diapered with painted work in outline or slight shading.

Groseing, the biting away the edge of the glass with pliers to make it fit. With regard to this word and to the term "calm," I have never found any one who could give a reason for the name or an authority as to its spelling, the various spellings suggested for the *latter* word including Karm, Calm, Carm, Kaim, and

172

even Qualm! But while writing this book I in lucky hour consulted the treatise of Theophilus, and was delighted to find both words. The term he applies to the leads is "Calamus" (a reed), while his term for what we should call pliers is "Grosarium ferrum" (groseing iron). So that this question is set at rest for ever. Glaziers must henceforth accept the classic spellings "Calm" and "Groseing," and one may suppose they will be proud to learn that these everyday terms of their craft have been in use for 900 years, and are older than Westminster Abbey.

Lath, the ruler, 3 to 8 feet long, and marked with inches, &c., used in setting out the "forms."

Lathykin, doubtless old English "a little lath," described p. 137.

Lasting-nails, described p. 141.

Leaf (of lead), the two uprights of the "H" section (fig. 34).

Muller, a piece of granite or glass, flat at the base, for grinding pigment, &c.

Obtuse, an angle having a wider opening than a right-angle or "perpendicular."

Orphreys (*aurifrigia*, from Lat. *aurum*, gold), the bands of ornament on ecclesiastical vestments.

Patina, the film produced on various substances by chemical action (oxidation, sulphurisation, &c.), either artificially, as in bronze sculpture, or by age, as in glass.

Plating, the doubling of one glass with another in the same lead.

Quarries, the diamond, square, or other shaped panes used in plain-glazing.

Reamy, wavy or streaky glass. (See p. 179.)

Scratch-card, a wire brush to remove tarnish from lead before soldering (p. 144).

Setting, fixing a charcoal or chalk drawing on the paper by means of a spray of fixative.

Shafting, see "Canopy."

Shooting (in carpentry), the planing down of an edge to get it truly straight.

Squaring-out, enlarging (or reducing) any design by drawing from point to point across proportional squares.

Stippling, described p. 100.

Stopping-knife, the knife by which the glass and lead are manipulated in leading-up.

Tabernacle work, see "Canopy."

Template, the form in paper, card, wood, or zinc, of *shaped* openings, by which the correct figure is set out on the cartoon-form.

THE END

Lightning Source UK Ltd.
Milton Keynes UK
UKOW051713250412

191444UK00002B/188/P